Praise for
That Which Transpires Behind That Which Appears

"We are fortunate to have a Sufi master like Pir Vilayat in the West. By offering this retreat book he gifts us a splendid treasury of practices, perspectives, and wisdom of the heart."

Jack Kornfield
co-founder of Insight Meditation Center
and Spirit Rock Meditation Center
author of *Bringing Home the Dharma*

"This book is a manual for self-transformation. Pir Vilayat has applied Sufi wisdom to the perplexities and stresses of modern life, informing his readers how to think clearly and live peacefully, while appreciating beauty and developing spiritually."

Stanley Krippner, PhD
professor of Psychology, Saybrook College
author of *The Mythic Path* and *Healing States*

"*That Which Transpires Behind That Which Appears* is as close to experiential learning as words in print could ever be. . . . Pir Vilayat Inayat Khan reflects a source and a mirror of peace."

Abdul Aziz Said
professor of International Relations
American University
founder, International Peace and Conflict Resolution
Division and Center for Global Peace

"A long-awaited compendium of wisdom from the great Sufi master Pir Vilayat Khan. His translation of the profound experience of Sufism into practical guidelines that sincere students can follow is a great contribution to the spiritual world."

Sri Swami Satchidananda
founder of Integral Yoga
author of *The Living Gita*

"Pir Vilayat uses words with healing magic to stimulate our growth and to entrain us in our growth to God. Fly home on his maps."

Rabbi Zalman Schachter-Shalom
professor, Naropa University and Temple University
founder of B'nai Or and Alliance for Jewish Renewal
author of *Jewish with Feeling* and *A Heart Afire*

"At long last, Pir Vilayat Inayat Khan's message is available in book form. Now we can ponder in written form what we have long valued in his spoken word: clear and strong images, detailed and eminently practical instructions. Behind that which appears on these pages transpires a fiery teacher, an agile mind, a voice that arouses the heart like music. May this book bring joy and new insights to countless readers."

Brother David Steindl-Rast
Benedictine monk
author of *Gratefulness, the Heart of Prayer*

"In a clear and straightforward manner Pir Vilayat describes the transformation of consciousness that is at the core of the spiritual journey. Pir Vilayat both unveils the mysteries of the path and provides the seeker with the tools, the exercises and practices to make the journey that is the heart's greatest secret."

Llewellyn Vaughan-Lee
founder of the Golden Sufi Center
author of *For Love of the Real*

Single Rye Grass. Photograph © Walter Chappell.

That which
TRANSPIRES
behind
That which
APPEARS

That which
TRANSPIRES
behind
That which
APPEARS

THE EXPERIENCE OF SUFISM

Pir Vilayat Inayat Khan

Sulūk Press
Richmond, Virginia

Published by Sulūk Press
an imprint of Omega Publications Inc.
Richmond, Virginia
www.omegapub.com

Cover image "Flammarion." Cover design by Sandra Lillydahl.

Photographs from the *Metaflors* series @ Walter Chappell and are used by arrangement with the artist. Duplication without written consent of the artist is prohibited.

This edition is printed on acid-free paper that meets ANSI standard X39–48.

Inayat Khan, Vilayat (1916–2004)
That Which Transpires Behind That Which Appears
The Experience of Sufism
Includes preface, introduction, glossary, index,
biographical note
1.Sufism
I. Inayat, Khan, Vilayat II.Title

Library of Congress Control Number: 2018946909

Printed and bound in the United States of America

ISBN 978-0-930872-49-6 paper edition

Contents

Milk Thistle. Photograph ©Walter Chappell.

Photographs by Walter Chappell

Editor's Preface

On the first weekend of March 1993, about one hundred people gathered for an intensive three-day spiritual retreat guided by Pir Vilayat Inayat Khan. The text of *That Which Transpires Behind That Which Appears* is composed of the edited transcripts of Pir Vilayat's teaching during that retreat weekend.

In preparing this material for publication, we have tried to remain as close to Pir Vilayat's actual words as possible, while being aware that the printed word is a different medium than the spoken word. The editing that has been done has been more a cutting away of extraneous material than of making additions.

In particular, we have not attempted to supplement the material in the transcripts of this retreat with material given by Pir Vilayat at other times, when he may have spoken on the same subject.

The text contains some words which are infrequently encountered, and Pir Vilayat uses some words in a deliberate but unusual manner. We have chosen to leave these words in the text, and to provide a glossary in which the meaning of such terms may be found.

There is, during the process of this style of retreat, something subtle but very real which is communicated by the tone of the teaching: an understanding that could deepen the overall experience, which comes through in the flow of ideas, rather than being contained only in the ideas.

In choosing to edit the material as we have, it is our hope that, should it be possible for such a sense of presence to be communicated through the printed pages of a book, it will seep through these pages into the reader's awareness.

The transcriptions of the recorded material were prepared by Mariel Walters and Abi'1-Khayr. Sharif Graham served as editorial consultant. The manuscript was proofread by Joan Claire Firozia Veriditas and Majida Gibson, each of whom made valuable suggestions. The primary editing of the text and the preparation of the notes, glossary, and bibliography have been by Abi'l Khayr.

There are many other people who, each in their own way, have made this publication possible. The author extends a heartfelt *thank you* to each of them.

The second edition was edited by Sandra Lillydahl and Cannon Labrie, with assistance from Pir Zia Inayat-Khan.

Introduction

Once, many years ago, I was undergoing one of the great tests that life sometimes offers us. Being young and quite vulnerable to the secret forces of my own mind, I found myself in a place of great confusion. Not knowing how to find my soul's teaching for me at that moment, I asked Pir Vilayat for some guidance and help. He shared with me a history of painful events in his own life and how he had allowed himself to use the retreat process to quiet his mind and allow the inner guidance to emerge.

Armed with this information and a list of various practices and meditations, I secluded myself in a tiny hut perched atop a mountain. This was to be my moment of truth, and I waited for the bolt of enlightenment to arrive and thrust me past all of the difficulties of my life and lead me to a place of clarity and wisdom. However, as each day passed I found myself sinking deeper and deeper into the sadness and pain of my own life.

The answer that I had hoped would arrive from within was not making itself heard to my mind. I diligently prayed, fasted, meditated, and performed those mini-rituals which one creates when on retreat.

The pain and confusion continued to be present, but also sharing my consciousness were the new states of detachment and an ecstatic feeling of reverie. My mind began to lighten, and there was a hidden memory trying to shine through the clouds of confusion.

Realizing one day that I was suddenly ravenously hungry, I decided to leave my world for a bit and find a slice of bread. I walked for forty-five minutes to a kitchen tent used by the people at a meditation camp that was occurring while I was on retreat. I saw no one, found my slice of bread, and returned to my hut.

As I sat there, slowly eating my bread, the realization of the depth of the inner world began to be experienced by my heart. Waves of profound joy washed over me, and the nature of my pain changed. No longer was it something to run from or root out, but instead it became an integral part of God's unfoldment in and through me.

In this state I knew the answer to my life's dilemma was available. I asked my soul for its guidance, and understood the answer through all the subtle layers of my ego. When I asked what I was to do, the answer was clear: Just keep doing what you are already doing

This clear answer was the one direction I had not considered in my quest for peace. Experiencing this idea in an awakened state of being gave it and me a new sense of vitality and purpose. Knowing Sufism to be based upon experience, I was waiting for an almost external experience of guidance, and had not remembered that true guidance is the inner light reflected on a still pond.

After having guided many retreats over the years, using the alchemical transformation model developed by Pir Vilayat Khan, I have come to see both the perfection and wisdom in this model. Sometimes the beginning of a retreat is overwhelming for both the guide and the retreatant. The guide must feel the burden of responsibility, and the retreatant apprehension that the retreat will not be successful in some way or other. The model provides a clear sense of boundary and also links the retreatant with a process that feels thousands of years old.

What Pir Vilayat has achieved in this book is the awakening of a sense in the reader of controlling one's own inner progress. The retreat is truly an alone process. Even the primary practice of zikr is awakening the state of knowing that nothing exists except God—a very lonely realization.

Yet, by experiencing that aloneness on the retreat, you realize that there is nobody other than yourself that can awaken you and deepen your compassion for self and others. Even your relationship with God becomes that of friend to friend. This is truly revolutionary for religion, but is the essence of the spiritual path.

Shahabuddin David Less

Bleeding Heart Leaf. Photograph ©Walter Chappell.

Invocation

We invoke the One
    whose body is the cosmos, which we share in
our bodies;
and whose mind is the software behind the
    existential appearance of reality, and in which
    mind we participate in our thinking;
and whose presence is continually lying in wait in
    our being, and yet who outstrips any concept that
    we can possibly construct.
And we invoke all those beings who have attained
    a level of realization that inspires us and helps us
    to validate our being and fulfill the purpose of
    our life.

Chapter 1

Guidelines for Retreat

We will, in the following pages, go through the stages of a spiritual retreat. The Sufis call this process *khalwa*.

First, a few introductory remarks about the format, the local environment, in which a retreat generally takes place. Perhaps the setting is not as comfortable as you would like but there is no pretense, no show: it is real. In fact, where there is too much comfort, or even opulence, there may be personal gain corning into the picture. Each of us has to sort this out in our own life.

Yet, one thing is clear: we cannot attain a state of ecstasy sitting in an armchair watching TV with our feet up, smoking a pipe or munching snack food. Or by going grudgingly to our job, hoping to get the maximum out of it with the least effort. Or, by trying to see what we can gain in life—that really will not do it for us.

On retreat we are seeking another dimension. We do not satisfy what people are looking for in the world, what is called "the world outside" in the Indian tradition. No, to discover the ability to unfurl the potentialities of your being you have to look inside. You have to scan the sky and brave the seasons. You have to feel precarious and vulnerable and, at the same time, test your mettle—so that you discover forces within your being that you never thought you had. Take up a challenge. Reach beyond the limits of your self-image and allow yourself to cry, to laugh, and to be part of all things, and yet find your own special being within the totality. See yourself in the universe, and see the universe in yourself. Discover yourself by becoming, by doing.

The retreat situation marks a halt in which we step out of our normal mode of existence in order to reflect upon our lives and gain more clarity and, ultimately, become more aware of what our real objective is in life. We want to attain illumination. We want to save our emotional attunement from the low-key condition into which it slips, and even from the somewhat vulgar emotions that we tend to slip into in our dealings with the social environment. And we want to be able to plug into what the dervishes call spiritual power, which will give us a sense of the purpose of our life.

This purpose reveals itself in serving the divine cause: ensuring orderliness against the chaos and defilement and entropy which plague our planet to such a dangerous degree that we are now living on an endangered planet. We are exposing our progeny to a world that will be even worse than the one in which we are living.

We have a responsibility. A retreat is an opportunity for a lot of reflection, a time to explore those skills which will open up faculties that we are not using and insights of which we are not aware. It is an opportunity to unleash the spiritual power that will enable us to fulfill the purpose of our lives. Rather than considering it a retreat from life, let us consider it a rehearsal for life. The consequence is that we will need to reverse many of the things that we are used to for a short while. We do this in the hope that this attunement will then permeate and percolate through our everyday life, so that it will always be there.

There are four guidelines which have been delineated by the Sufis: silence, solitude, fasting, and watchfulness. The observance of these guidelines will make all the difference in a retreat. You could even say they make a retreat.

The first is silence, which contrasts with our everyday chatting. We are used to thinking in terms that enable us to explain what we are thinking because we are talking all the time. Our mind gets into a certain pattern. It thinks in a certain explicate manner in order to be able to convey—even when we are not talking to another, to convey to ourselves, to our limited minds— what our understanding tells us. If we are on silence, we do not have to prepare our minds for how we are going to explain what we are experiencing. We also do not have to try to convince our middle-range mind about what we have discovered.

Consequently, we discover a whole dimension of thinking that is incredibly rich and which we never encompass in our middle-range thinking. Here we will discover two modes: one is the kind of thinking that we discover as we turn within, and the other is the kind of thinking that we discover as we shift our consciousness upward, as it were, into the transcendental dimension.

A few introductory words could give a sense of what that would mean: turning within is like seeing how the impressions of the outer world enrich us as we ingest them in our being. In this process, the impressions are transmuted, so that just the quintessence of them is incorporated in our being. But, to pursue this further, during the process of digesting we do have to reject those impressions that we cannot digest. We reject them at the surface, let us say toward the earth, vertically, as the immune system does.

But there is also a relatively unknown function that takes place whereby what we have ingested gets resorbed into the void and recycled. David Bohm speaks of forms unfolding from what he terms the holomovement, and being enfolded again within this holomovement, a dance between the explicate state and the implicate state that is happening all the time.[1]

In a retreat we are highlighting both aspects of ourselves: the aspect whereby the way the world looks in the explicate format is integrated, or digested, as it is transmuted into the implicate condition; and then the opposite is also true that, having done this, now we act upon the environment from within instead of from the surface of our being.

It makes all the difference, because most of us are simply reacting to the situations outside us without calling upon all the resourcefulness in our being. Whereas, if we learn how to turn within we are able to call upon and to awaken all those inner faculties. You could say that it makes for a greater efficiency in adding value to our being rather than gaining material well-being. It is in terms of realization.

The difference between this and awakening in what we might call the transcendental dimension would be like shifting from trying to sort through the hardware to starting to explore the nature of the software. It would be like being able to rise at will from your earthly condition and grasp what is being enacted behind

1 David Bohm, *Wholeness and the Implicate Order*, 150–57.

the physical world. We will discover that we exist on several planes and that, in most people, the communications between these planes have been broken. We are not complete until we are able to integrate all levels of our being.

This leads to discovering that space only has meaningfulness where there is matter. The mind is involved in bodiness, as in certain mental functions which are connected with the body. But there are mental functions that are not connected with the body. And that is why Jalal ad-Din Rumi said: "I walk without feet and fly without wings, and I see without eyes and hear without ears."[2] And I would add, "I think without a brain." A brain is a limitation to our thinking. It is a very useful tool but let us not be bogged-in by the tool.

The software of the universe is a reality whether it is ever explicated and activated into hardware or not. It still is a reality. So let us not confine our minds to our bodies. You could discover your being irrespective of your body and irrespective of your mind. If you are reading this book, it is likely that you are seeking something beyond the middle range. These are the things we are going to work with.

To start with, we want to recognize something very basic: we are pulled. There is no way of explaining this logically, but we are actually being pulled in two directions in our lives—what seem to be two opposite directions. On one side, we feel a need to build a beautiful world of beautiful people. That is, to improve our physical conditions, to improve ourselves by more learning and more understanding, to cultivate a beautiful

2 Jalal ad-Din Rumi (1207–73) famed Persian Sufi poet of Konya and founder of the Mawlawi (Mevlevi) Order.

manner. That is all part of building a beautiful world of beautiful people.[3]

The other pull exercised upon our being is a need for freedom. This is a need we are not always clear about, although it shows itself very clearly in our lives. Ultimately, it is a need for freedom from conditioning. To quote Hazrat Pir-o-Murshid Inayat Khan, those things that we are attached to become, in time, burdens.[4]

In order to build a beautiful world of beautiful people we get involved in situations and relations with people in which our freedom is limited. Yet we need to find an inner freedom. The only way to reconcile these two pulls upon us is to reconcile the irreconcilables, to find an inner freedom while involving ourselves outwardly to the extent of limiting our freedom but, we would caution, accepting the limits caused by our involvement with the world with some discretion, and with a clear knowledge of what is going on.

There are several stages in the acquisition of freedom. One stage is freedom from what we imagine the physical world to be. The image that we make of the physical world is totally off, but we do not realize it—we are so convinced that it is the way that we see it. More importantly, we are so convinced our problems are what we think they are. We so easily get entangled by our assessment of our problems.

3 It is said that God is beautiful and loves beauty (Hadith). If, then, the manifestation is viewed as an attempt to satisfy the divine wish, it follows that our purpose is to build a beautiful world of beautiful people—in other words, to become the expression of the divine wish for beauty.

4 Hazrat Inayat Khan, *The Art of Being and Becoming*, 122. "Pir-o Murshid" or "Murshid" used here and throughout this book refers to Inayat Khan (1882–1927), Pir Vilayat's father and the person who first brought Sufism to the West.

All problems are, ultimately, problems of relationship. There is a way of involving oneself with people so as to free them from themselves, instead of seeking an outward freedom oneself. It is very, very subtle. It would mean looking for interdependence rather than independence or, on the other hand, codependence. As the Sufis say: renounce the world, renounce yourself, and then renounce renunciation—out of love.[5] That is not the way of the sannyasins, who typically are seeking illumination for themselves.

This happens right in life. What we want to do is to unmask the hoax of our ordinary assumptions: that the physical world is the way we think it is, and that our problems are what we think they are. Only then will we start grasping what is being enacted behind our problems.

In the Sufi practices we are trying to grasp more clearly what we call the divine names, which are the names of God (*asma ilahi*). What is intended by these practices is to be able to earmark the qualities in the universe that manifest and actuate themselves in our personality. These are the issues behind our dramas, this is what is being enacted: whether this quality or that quality comes through or is being hindered by our behavior; or hindered by our lack of grasping its significance, or its meaningfulness, or its relevance in a particular situation.

We need also to consider freedom from opinion. We are so convinced about our opinion—that is why people go to war. The superstition and ignorance found in the opinions of people cause so much suffering in the

---

5 Attributed to Farid ad-Din 'Attar (1145–1220), author of *The Conference of the Birds.*

world. We involve our ego in our opinion, we do not want to be proved wrong. Freedom from opinion involves freedom from the ego, freedom from the wish to dominate.

You can see that this is the path of selflessness instead of mastery. Seeking freedom is the path of the saints.

Freedom from our opinions is going to lead us toward freedom from the prison of our self-image. We are convinced that we are the person that we think we are, and consequently we can never evolve. We can never change if we think we are what we think we are; we get encapsulated in this notion of ourselves. Perhaps one of the clues to this is to realize that we are wearing a mask and playing a role, and, as Pir-o-Murshid says, the king thinks he is a king because he is sitting on the throne and people say "your majesty."[6] But if they did not, he would not think he is the king. We think we are a baby or an old man or a woman or whatever, but that is just the outer aspect, the self-image: it is just an illusion covering a deeper reality.

We say we want to know who we are. Yes. According to Sufis, we will have to peel away 22,000 veils until we find who we are. Freedom, then, from our self-image.

Then we seek freedom from personal emotions that bog us down, such that we miss participation in the cosmic celebration in the heavens. We have to work on this area of personal emotions, but we must not be dogmatic in categorizing, making a difference between divine emotion and human emotion. Think, rather, of a continuum, with human emotion at one extreme and divine emotion at the other. Of course, there are transi-

---

6 *The Vision of God and Man*, vol. 12, *The Sufi Message of Hazrat Inayat Khan*, 142.

tory conditions all along the way. Sometimes it is good to have an illustration, a model to help us understand ourselves. You could think of yourself as a pyramid upside down, so that at the bottom we are an individual and at the top we are the totality. We are the whole pyramid. At every transitional stage between those two extremes we are just like, for example, the fragment of a hologram that carries the potentiality of the whole hologram within it.

Our thinking of ourselves as individuals is going to alienate us from the infinite dimension of our being. We are standing in the way of our own unfoldment by the kind of concept that we make of ourselves. This goes further than just freedom from our self-image. This is really freedom from our notion of being an individuality.

The freedom that embraces all these modes, or levels, of freedom, is freedom from conditioning. These were the words of Buddha at the moment of illumination after the forty-nine days of retreat: "I have freed myself from determinism, conditioning." You realize that people brought up in certain social environments are Muslim or Christian or Jew; that in a certain environment you think a certain way, in another environment you think in another way. It can be difficult to realize the degree to which your own thinking is conditioned.

We have to explore our thinking carefully because it leads us into perspectives in which we are caught in a bind, just as under the effect of a drug one is caught in a bind. We are seeking freedom from any kind of bind, and, therefore, we will have to be very clear as to how our thinking is conditioned and how we can deprogram it, as it were, and find freedom. It is not just our thinking: our emotions, too, are conditioned.

It is through our creativity that we are able to free ourselves from determinism—that is, if our creativity is genuine and spontaneous, truly inventive, and not simply a replicate of the environment. The environment can be the catalyst that is going to release our potentialities, but we must not think that all we need to do is release potentialities that are there. We create them as we actuate them.

We need to reverse a lot of assumptions that we, perhaps surreptitiously, have learned. It is good to question the points of view and the assumptions that you learn. We are trying as far as possible to free ourselves from traditional ways of thinking in order to explore the spirituality of the future.

There are new ways of looking at things. Instead of assuming that we have to conform to a pre-established harmony, as Leibniz called it, consider that we create orderliness out of disorder.[7] It is our incentive that creates order. Or, let us say that there is an impending orderliness in the universe buried under the disorderliness at the surface, which can only manifest through the exercising of our free will. We create the path by freeing it, instead of following an asphalt road that has been predetermined for us by our society. We have to be pioneers, to brave the unknown. Do away with our crutches. The pull of the future is stronger than the push of the past. We are to be created as we go along.

We cannot rest upon the knowledge that has been communicated to us from tradition. We have to know it and, knowing it, we are to move forward. Burn our

7 For a discussion of Leibniz's pre-established harmony and its implications see Ira Progoff, *Jung, Synchronicity, and Human Destiny: Non-Causal Dimensions of Human Experience*, chap. 6.

boats. That is why Pegasus was unable to reach Olympus. Bellerophon, as the rider, had to make the rest of the journey himself and not rely upon the support system that is offered by the earth.[8] You are on your own. Trust yourself to the self-organizing faculty that is in you and that explores new ways of being.

So, we are being pulled in two directions. One is to achieve, to fulfill our objective to build a beautiful world of beautiful people. The kind of emotion behind this is, according to the Sufis, *'ishq Allah*, which is nostalgia, a quest for joy. But we are also pulled in the opposite direction, to seek freedom from involvement at all the different levels we have been considering. The emotion behind it is peace rather than joy.

The Sufis provide a model that could be useful to us in this situation. According to them, as God exhales, God manifests and actuates the latent possibilities within God's own Being, and thereby finds fulfillment. The springhead behind this is 'ishq Allah, the power of love. It was not in order to know the divine Self that God created the universe, it was out of love for the possibility of you that God descended from the solitude of unknowing.[9]

---

8 Pegasus, the winged horse, is said to represent nature and instinct; the release of this earthy energy is not sufficient, the myth would seem to say, to reach Olympus, the home of the gods. See Erich Neumann, *The Origins and History of Consciousness*, 217–19. An interesting parallel is found in the Miraj of the Prophet Muhammad, in which the horse Buraq carries him in his ascent toward heaven. Inayat Khan states, "The Buraq could not go beyond a certain point, which means that breath takes one a certain distance in the mystical realization, but there comes a stage when the breath cannot accompany one." *Song of the Prophets*, 255.

9 The source of this statement may be derived from the views

When we exhale—this is the Sufi way of doing the practices—we consider our breath as the extension of the divine breath that is pursuing its objective; that is, as it manifests and actuates potentialities that would otherwise remain latent or virtual. Our pursuit of excellence in life is an expression of the divine nostalgia coming—well, not coming through us, because then we would be thinking in terms of duality—but we are that very quest for fulfillment. We are it. We have to think in terms of unity rather than duality.

As we inhale, then, we participate in the divine inhaling whereby God withdraws, or extracts, the quintessence of what has been gained in terms of wisdom from the existential world. This wisdom gets recycled into the software of the universe. In order to enrich the totality, that which has been gained by our experience and by our personality must first be distilled. It is the quintessence of what we have gained in terms of understanding that contributes toward the reprogramming of the whole universe.

Instead of thinking in terms of separation—God and ourselves—consider that we participate in the divine understanding, we contribute toward it. Think of God dynamically instead of statically. God as us, yet beyond any fragmentation.

In order to be clear what we mean by distilling the quintessence of the knowledge that we have gained, we could give some examples: a doctor would learn technical things about the human body, about medicines and their effects; a carpenter would learn about the nature

---

of al-Hallaj and Ibn 'Arabi. See Louis Massignon, *The Passion of al-Hallaj*, trans. Herbert Mason, and Henry Corbin, *Creative Imagination in the Sufism of Ibn Arabi*, Henry Corbin.

of wood, how it reacts to its formative process; a musician would learn about the different instruments in the orchestra, and different scales and rhythms.

But what would be the quintessence of this knowledge? The kind of insight that the doctor has about the nature of life, or that the musician has about the way that meaningfulness and emotion can be translated into structures. The kind of knowledge of matter that a good carpenter, or particularly a cabinetmaker, would develop. The know-how that the farmer discovers in working with and fructifying the earth—there are technical aspects of it, such as knowing when certain seeds should be sown, but the quintessential aspect of this knowledge can never be defined in categories. It is a tangible sense of the energy of the earth.

It is this quintessence of the knowledge gained through experience, through know-how, that is recycled into the programming of the universe. This allows the universe to progress, which it does by mutating and evolving. We contribute toward it, and there you see the purpose of your life.

It is very important for us to see the relevance of our lives in relationship with the universe. Instead of thinking of ourselves as a fragment of the universe, we could think of ourselves as being a focus of the totality, the convergence of the totality, and having a contribution toward that totality. What we want to do is to gain realization, and that realization has to do with our relationship with the universe as a whole.

Many of the practices that we have been doing in the past were Yoga practices. For example, by becoming aware of your breathing you slow down your breathing. That shifts your consciousness from the catabolic to the anabolic condition—your whole physical metabolism, your mental metabolism, your energy levels. In this practice, you do, somewhat unwittingly, intervene in the rhythm of your breath with your will. The Sufi way is, instead of thinking "I am breathing in," or "I am breathing out," or "I am holding my breath," to think that it is God breathing. If you prefer, you could say that it is the whole universe ebbing and flowing. What you think is your breath is just like a wave in the ocean. It is just the way the ebb and flow of cosmic energy is being customized as you.

This perspective will make a significant difference in your breathing practice. What is more, you will be able to breathe much more slowly without imposing your will artificially upon your breathing process. You are taking advantage of this wonderful, very primary function to gain realization. It is not just a physical practice.

As you exhale, be aware of what you are doing in life, of your efforts to improve conditions. Instead of thinking that you are doing it, consider that the whole thrust of the universe, moved by 'ishq Allah, is endeavoring to build a beautiful world of beautiful people. Think of it in detail: for instance, you would like to improve your house and your garden, your knowledge of art and music, improve yourself—very concrete examples.

That thinking is from the individual vantage point. But if you feel the whole nostalgia of the universe coming through, and that you are the expression of that— the nostalgia of the universe is carried further as your wish—then you will not feel that you are at logger-heads with God. You will feel a great power coming through you. Or, rather, you will discover yourself as power. There is still a tendency to think in terms of duality, whereas it is all one. What you think is your power is the divine power that gets funneled, and therefore limited, and even distorted and defiled.

So, feel the divine power that orders things in an orderly way, as opposed to randomness. This is the way, for example, to build a beautiful house: bringing orderliness where otherwise things would be just sloppy and slaphappy. That is the pursuit of excellence.

As you inhale, discover in yourself what in India is called a sannyasin, and *vairagya*—which means the kind of detachment and indifference such that you are not dependent upon prevailing circumstances for your joy, or for your realization, or for your unfoldment. As Pir-o-Murshid said: "Indifference and independence are the two wings that enable the soul to fly."[10]

This again is the personal dimension. In the divine perspective everything is integrated into a totality, whereas in a chaotic state things are unrelated. There is a movement toward integration in the universe which requires the quintessentiation of the essence of what is achieved. This means the contingent underpinning must fall apart, or fall away. So as you inhale, you are letting go of a lot of things that you may have become dependent upon, and it is your consequent freedom that is going to enable you to participate in this quintessentiation of all that has been achieved in life.

Behind your quest for detachment and indifference is something very profound, which is the divine unifying function. You feel the divine unity. Do not confuse solitude with loneliness. There is a solitary aspect to our being which you will find during a retreat; you find your own space. Whereas, when you are continually

10 Hazrat Inayat Khan, *The Complete Sayings*, 19.

sharing with other people you tend to lose sight of your own special vibration or atmosphere.

That is the second guideline for a retreat. The first one is silence. The second one is solitude. It goes together with detachment.

The third one is fasting. Well, it is much more than that. It really means freeing yourself from any kind of dependence—including, of course, addiction—but dependence upon any kind of support whatsoever. In other words, you drop your crutches.

The fourth guideline is what the mystics call watches in the night. That is the outer format. The inner one is being continually aware and awake. You find that you do not enjoy sleeping as much. You tend to wake up in the middle of the night and want to meditate—not because you are told you have to do it, but you just have that need to follow up your awakening by shaking away your slumber and becoming very aware.

Chapter 2

Intuition

Avail yourself of the opportunity that a spiritual re-treat offers to do some really constructive work. You need to work very, very clearly with your consciousness and your thinking, building it step by step, further and further, until you reach into wider dimensions. You do not want simply to go off into the blue somewhere and lose your handle, your grip. This is something that does happen in spiritual groups, with the consequence that you become otherworldly and unable to relate what you are discovering to the fulfillment of your purpose in life. With small steps, therefore, we will be systematically building from scratch.

It is not good enough just to assume that things are maya. That would be the negative aspect of it; the positive would be to ask: "But what are they?" It is not good enough to say, "It is all maya and I am letting myself be fooled." What it requires is some rather tedious work. If you want to play the piano, it would be nice to start off playing some Chopin or Brahms. But you would play it better if first you worked more on your scales. Pablo Casals used to work on his scales every morning for an hour or an hour and a half.

So, if it is tedious we apologize. But we need to do that groundwork, and then we will gradually build upon it—perhaps reaching points when our consciousness reaches right up into the heavens. What it really means is that we have to adapt our minds in order to provide a solid foundation for our realization. Otherwise there is a conflict there, a contradiction.

In a lot of schools the student begins with practices of concentration. If you follow Yoga, for example, the *Yoga Sutra* of Patanjali start with breathing practices and physical exercises called *asanas*. Then you start building up by concentrating on an object. You look at an object for twenty minutes without scanning the object, that is, without moving your glance, shifting your glance, from one aspect of the object. Eventually you find that the object seems to be floating in space.

This is an interesting experiment. You realize to what extent your glance shifts continually unless you exercise control of it. In experiments with sleep in laboratories it has been found that when we are dreaming the eyes are moving in what is called rapid eye movement. You can see the relationship between the motion of your eyes and the focus of your thoughts.

You start by working with an object, and eventually just a point; for example, you place a nail in the wall and you concentrate on that nail for an hour or two. We are, however, so used to using our very active minds that we find this method does not honor the natural dynamism of the mind. We would rather use methods which encourage our creativity. So we are going to suggest themes of meditation which are very grounded, but which will give us a little more scope for our minds.

It is not good to kill our minds, or even to constrain them. Rather, we want to guide them and give them a direction. What is more, our lives and our problems are a very good object of meditation—rather than choosing an artificial object from our mantelpiece. Based in our own life situations, meditation will not lead us to otherworldliness but will give us a clearer insight into our lives, and help us to fulfill our purpose. This kind of meditation is in keeping with the way of the Sufis, who value life rather than seeking an escape from life.

What we are suggesting is that we start with perception, or at least a representation of perception. Then we will use that as an illustration of what is happening to our mind. We will be building up step-by-step, and eventually it will become inspiring.

Imagine that you are looking at a vast panorama. It could be a scene in nature, with a lot of things that you are trying to perceive at the same time. Your capacity to encompass all this is overstressed, and as a consequence you cannot quite relate the different elements in that panorama. Like, for example, when we used to attend cinemas that had three screens: instead of the films presenting us with separate scenes, they presented us with a lot of scenes at the same time. As a consequence, our sight would pan because it was unable to grasp, to interrelate, all the bounty in front of our eyes.

This is what we are doing with our minds all the time. We are dealing with a lot of ideas that are not related, and, therefore, our attention is scattered.

We are going to forestall, to prefigure, what we are trying to get at; and then we will move through the steps leading to it. We are trying to get at the state of the mind in which we develop intuition. That is, the state of the mind in which thoughts that apparently seem unrelated all of a sudden make sense; all of a sudden you see a relationship between them that you did not see before. That is intuition.

These are the steps leading to that state of mind. What we suggest is that when you are faced, as we are most of the time, with a lot of thoughts, that you consider each package of thoughts in turn. You know the mind works by what is called association. Perhaps you think of a flower, and that reminds you of someone who gave you a flower, and that reminds you of another person, and then you think of a friend of that person—and so on. The mind just skips off all over the place, randomly, by the process of association. That is what happens in dreams; there is no control with the mind.

So, the first thing is to take a thought, rather than an object, and resist the temptation to skip off all over the place. Choose an example from your life, a situation in your life that involves another person. Take the time to become very clear about that situation, and notice how you are involved. What it means in terms of your relationship with the person. What the consequences are in your relationship with people who are related to that person. What the consequences are in terms of your future plans, and so on. There are a lot of implications, but always come back to the main thought—just like a music student studying composition might be instructed to make variations on a theme, yet advised to continually come back to that theme.

Do this for a short while.

Can you see how your mind keeps meandering all over the place? And, gently but firmly, you bring it back.

Now to make one step further. Remember what our objective is: accessing the state of mind in which we develop intuition. This will be the next step. First of all, the perceptual image. We are going to relate two scenes, nature scenes, that are in some way related although different. And we are going to learn how to toggle between one scene and the other. They could be part of the same scene. For example, you could imagine a mountain and a lake. Either you concentrate on the mountain or you concentrate on the lake, and you keep on alternating between the two. You can, instead of toggling between one and the other, you can combine them in a composite picture. That seems simple enough.

So we take one more step forward. Think of a scene in which there is a tree, and then there is a background. There could be mountains in the background. If you are taking photographs, for example, there could be the person you are photographing and then there is the background. You can focus in such a way as to highlight that person, and have the background fade in the distance; or you could take what would normally not be considered a good photograph, with the person out of focus but the background in focus. You see how, once more, you can toggle between two perspectives.

Now let us apply this to our dealing with our life situations. There would be many ways of doing it, but we will make it a little more specific. Think of a situation in your life at present; then think of a situation in your childhood, or earlier in your life, which bears some resemblance with your present situation. You realize that life seems to repeat itself. The same pattern seems to reproduce itself, unless you can recognize the pattern. Therefore, the reminiscence of a situation from your past similar to the one you are in now is going to throw light on your situation now. And, your situation now will help you understand that situation from the past.

These are steps toward realization. You are beginning to see something that you had not seen before. That knowledge is going to free you from being subject to conditioning, even if it is a condition of habit. That is what we are seeking.

In these practices we start by toggling, that is, alternating between one view and the other one, until we see a connection between them. We could even superimpose them one upon the other. For example, perhaps you have looked in the mirror and have seen the difference between your face when you are thinking with resentment or anger toward a person who has offended you, and your face at the moment when you have found joy and peace in yourself. It is the same face but different expressions. Again, you could toggle between the two; and since there is some similarity between them you can superimpose them. You toggle, but the images are very, very close.

You begin to see something deeper than the differences. You see your real being behind the different facets of your being. You find the unity behind the diversity.

This could lead us to a little more sophisticated practice. Perhaps you have seen the hologram with which you can shift your perspective such that in one perspective you see the Shroud of Turin of Christ, and then in another perspective one sees a painting of Christ. It just takes a little bit to shift your consciousness from one image to the other. If those images are very different then there is no way in which you can successfully superimpose them. But if they are similar you will find that, indeed, you do not have to toggle you can see something in common there.

This will lead us into a further dimension of our understanding. As Pir-o-Murshid says: a wave is a condition of the sea.[1] It is not reality *sui generis*, as one says in Latin, it is not a reality that is independent of its ground. Think of yourself as being more like the ocean than the waves. Consider your present condition as a condition of God rather than your condition, even as a temporary condition of God which can eventually be dissolved. But the reality behind it is eternal.

Try to grasp the difference between the surface of your being that is transient and mortal and subject to dissolution, and the essence of your being that is permanent. It is not like separating beans from peas: you are not separating two different things. It is discovering the continuity in change, and highlighting the continuity instead of highlighting the change. You begin to discover a dimension of your being entirely different from the one with which you normally identify.

You could do the same thing, and bring it more into focus, when watching your thoughts. You can grasp something more fundamental in your thoughts than the way they appear at the surface of your understanding. In order to convey what we are thinking we limit our thinking into discrete thoughts which are like categories, like a kind of granulation, and which miss the relevance, the overall context. So we get right into the explicate way of looking at the world where everything is made up of objects that are separated from each other

---

1 *Philosophy, Psychology, Mysticism*, vo. 11, *The Sufi Message of Hazrat Inayat Khan*, 68.

by a kind of skin, whereas in the deeper thinking we see the unity behind all things.

For example, if you are walking in the forest you feel the forest rather than the individual trees. You are accessing a deeper level of thinking. We could say it is that which we imply behind that which we explain. It is the implicit instead of the explicit. When you say something you imply a lot of things. You are not always aware of what you imply. Now, as we turn within, we are beginning to encompass wide expanses of thinking. We can see that our thoughts are simply derivations from that wide field, and that we let ourselves be captured by our mental constructs and miss the relevance behind it, the context.

We are shifting our thinking inward. The physical world such as it appears outside can be reached from inside, but you have to shift your mode altogether. The way that you can do it is to try to see how things look from the point of view of another person. Instead of imagining that person sitting in their room and you having a conversation with them, you imagine how that person thinks, how that person feels. You really get into the consciousness of that person. You could even experience how you appear to that person.

Instead of closing the doors to the outer world in order to turn within, the more you turn within, the more you must reach outside; but you reach outside from inside. If you do not do that, if you do not reach out, then you get encapsulated in your own psyche, in your storms in your teacups, as it is said in England. You are observing your thoughts just like you observe objects, and, exactly as you are deceiving yourself in your assessment of objects, in the same way you are deceiving yourself in your assessment of your thoughts. That is a dangerous way to go. Meditation does have dangerous aspects.

So, as soon as you start turning your consciousness inward, reach out from inside. The best way of doing this is to get into the consciousness of another person: to imagine—because we have that faculty of imagining—what it would be like to be that person. Then you will be able to understand the behavior of that person towards you.

That person deals with you on the assumption that you are what that person thinks you are, which is not what you are. But that explains why people do not understand you. Or, that is why people are behaving toward you in a totally incongruous way: it does not fit in with the representation that you have of yourself.

This is not thought-reading, and it is not telepathy. It would be an indiscretion to do that.

Of course, we also have to take into consideration the transcendental dimension. For example, getting into the consciousness of that person if that person were in a high state of meditation. It is helpful to practice this by concentrating on what we call a teacher, or a saint, or a prophet. (We are using the word *teacher* now instead of *master*, because the word *master* has some chauvinistic connotations.) This will help us discover a further dimension of our being, if we are able to get into the consciousness of beings who are more realized than ourselves.

Actually, this practice uncovers a realization that is already latent within us but which we do not acknowledge. We cannot make use of it because it is dormant. It is awakened by discovering the affinity—the only way to get into the consciousness of another person is by affinity, by resonance. Instead of thinking of the person as other, you resonate with that person. You discover the same thing in yourself that is present in that person. It seems very presumptuous to think that we have the same in us as very highly realized beings, but we do—it is just a matter of discovering it.

In order to attain realization you will find it helpful to be very clear about the difference between the way things look outside and the way that things look inside. There is a relationship there, it is not totally one or the other. There is some relationship. As an example, consider the difference between swimming at the surface of the lake and seeing the separate lotus flowers, or then swimming under the surface and seeing that these flowers are part of a network. There is a difference. On the surface you just see the separate flowers, while in the depth you see the interrelations between them. That will give you some kind of idea, a model, about the difference between outside and inside.

Once more, you need to toggle between the two instead of just screening yourself from the way the world looks from outside. The danger of doing that is that you get encapsulated in your psyche. The lotus flowers and the roots provide a very good example with which to work. Toggle between the two. Imagine that you are swimming at the surface and you see the separate flowers, and then you are swimming underneath and you see the interconnection.

Now think of your life. In your external way of looking at things you see people, problems, and situations as discrete entities, and your thoughts are also seen as discrete thoughts. As you turn within you see that they are all related to one another in a kind of network. But you get so overwhelmed by the bounty in that network that everything seems much more in focus when you get back into your external way of experiencing or of seeing things.

What you do as you turn within is very similar to how the eyes function. Each eye has a slightly different vision of the environment due to what is called parallax, but somehow the brain is able to extrapolate between these two pictures. Since there is no way in which we can fit these two pictures into a two-dimensional space, we imagine it as a space that is three-dimensional.

In the same way, we see the situations in our life as different, each as a distinct situation. As we turn within, our mind is able to see a relationship between those situations and build a composite picture. You begin to see the relationship between two situations that had seemed rather independent. Perhaps the most dire example of this would be what Jung indicated when he said if you do not confront your shadow you will find it coming to you in the form of your fate.[2] Notice the relationship. We normally do not see that relationship. We do not see how changing ourselves is going to change our problems. We think that our problems are in some way programmed by our destiny.

It is very difficult to accept that we call our problems to us. We think, rather, that our problems are inflicted upon us. Perhaps we can more easily see the connection if we discover that there are potentialities in our being that are continually trying to unfurl, and that the situations

---

2 "That which we do not bring to consciousness appears in our lives as fate." Carl Jung.

in our lives are connected with the way that these idio-syncrasies unfurl.

Let us be a little more specific. To become a wonder-ful being, all of the qualities that are present within you would have to be greatly enhanced. You would be full of joy, and compassion, and mastery, and all the qualities that you can imagine. Take one quality—for example, compassion—and then consider a problem in your life. See how you are being challenged in your compassion, and, by modifying your behavior in life, you will enhance the impact of your compassion on the situation. The situation becomes the means by which you unfurl the qualities of your being.

You can do this with all the different qualities. Truthful-ness. Mastery. There is a quotation from Caesar: sovereign-ty is a power that one loses by not using it. See the re-lationship there. We are trying to relate the inner with the outer because these qualities seem to emerge from a kind of vacuum in the center of our being—just like the fresh petals inside a flower emerge from within, and the jaded petals fall away so that the new petals may replace them. But this whole thing is related to your activities in daily life. It does not just happen of itself. There is always a relation there.

This leads us to the clue to intuition: everything is related to everything else in the mechanism of the uni-verse, but we do not always see it. In fact, we hardly ever see it. There is a better chance that we see it when we turn within. If we turn outside, we think of each event as separate. As we turn within, we collate the dif-ferent events into a composite whole, something which we can grasp, just like the perceptions of the two eyes are collated by the brain. If you turn within, your mind thinks differently. It is able to superimpose thoughts that are remotely related and that you could not connect when you were thinking in the explicate mode—that is, the way you think when you are considering the world as it appears from outside. This has enormous consequences leading to intuition. This is the clue to intuition.

Now, let us make one further step. Imagine that you were to photograph the fish in an aquarium to make a film. You have two cine cameras and you make two films simultaneously, from opposite sides of the aquarium and with the fish in the center. Then you view these films, and the two films would be different. Yet you would see that there is some commonality between them. In fact, complementarity. An example of that is again found in the words of Pir-o-Murshid Inayat Khan: think of what appeared to be a defeat that avers itself to be a victory.[3] Complementarity. What appears to be a victory avers itself to be a defeat. The last will be the first and the first will be the last—the words of Christ.[4] Things may turn out quite different from what we think.

Complementarity teaches us to always view things from the antipodal position compared to our personal point of view. The ultimate way of doing it is one of the features of the Sufi path: consider everything from the divine point of view and from your individual point of view, both simultaneously. In doing the breathing practices you are trying to see how things look from the divine point of view. Think of yourself as an extension of the

---

3 "Sometimes success is a defeat and defeat is a success." *Gayan, Vadan, Nirtan*, 156.
4 Matthew 20:16.

divine being—that is a clue to realization. Otherwise, you are simply limited by your own personal vantage point. It is so obvious, it is surprising that you find this level of realization so rarely. The extent to which people are caught in their personal vantage point is quite incredible.

This is the secret of the sacredness that we are seeking, but there is no way in which it makes any sense except if looked upon as the divine condition prior to its defilement in the existential world. Complementarity is always a challenge to our mind. Yet, a rotten peach is still a peach. It is all the being of God; yes, but it has been defiled, corrupted at its jagged ends. Dynamically, it is continually renewing itself.

Perhaps the most beautiful complementarity is the donkey participating in the glory of Christ, because there were laurels under its feet and it heard "Hosannas!" around its ears.[5] That part of us which is broken is glorified in the heavens. That was the message of Christ. We learn not to go according to our commonplace experience any more. A Rolls-Royce would not have made Christ any more important. Complementarity.

Now let us move a little further. You see a light, in your perception you see a light; and when you turn within you think you see a light. If you do that then you are being fooled because you are used to thinking in terms of perceiving. The only way to turn within without fooling yourself is to realize that you have to altogether give up the format of being the subject who is experiencing an object other than itself. You have to realize that in the inner world, or the implicate state,

---

5 Matthew 21:1–9.

what you think is the light that you see is the light that sees, not the light that can be seen.

If, indeed, as you turn within everything is interspersed—and all of our practices have led toward that conclusion, that everything is interspersed with everything else, just like radio waves—then light cannot be radiated from a source. We are talking about a different kind of light, not the kind of light that can be radiated from a source. We are talking about what Pir-o-Murshid calls the all-pervading light. If you think of yourself as that light—let us call it the light of intelligence—then your aura will burn more brightly. Whereas, if you try to radiate your aura more it will not have much effect. See the relationship between the inside and the outside.

We are training our minds to extrapolate between elements that seem different. We have seen that when these elements are very similar, like the views of the two eyes, then it is easier to extrapolate between them. When they are very different then we can only toggle between them, we cannot superimpose them. Our concentration can pass from one to the other, but we cannot quite see the relationship between them because they are too different. The great art of turning within is to see the connections between things that do not seem to be connected.

We are training our minds to arrive at great clarity as to how we can shift our thinking from the ordinary way of thinking. Suppose that the sun and the moon were in the position of eclipsing. Either the sun is eclipsing the moon or the moon is eclipsing the sun. They are aligned, but they are only aligned from the point of view of Planet Earth. So you see a connection between things from your point of view.

But there is a broader connection there. They can be aligned when they are not in alignment from the point of view of Earth. They can be in alignment from some other point in space, but we do not see that connection. We would have to be able to move our consciousness from our personal vantage point in order to see that connection. That is why, as we turn within, our vantage point is spread out from inside. It is not focalized as it is when we are looking at the physical environment. It becomes cosmic.

We can train ourselves by consistently questioning if things are the way we think they are; and by making an effort to depart from our personal vantage point in order to see a connection hidden from our personal vantage point. That is what Buddha called questioning your opinion. Questioning your opinion is not good enough. You still have to have that *aha!* moment. Questioning your opinion is going to release you, to free you from your personal vantage point. But the next thing is to be able to see how things could look from an alternate point of view. This leads you toward what is called awakening, which Pir-o-Murshid described as imagining that you are awake amongst a lot of people who are all asleep—and imagine that you remember having been asleep also and now you are awake. You see that everything is quite different from the way that you thought it was before. For example, Murshid says, imagine that you are watching a theater show in the evening and then the next morning you see the faces of the people without makeup, and you realize that they look quite different from the way they appeared. You realize that their castles were made of cardboard. That is the unreality of life which strikes you, and then the reality behind it begins to manifest, to appear, to transpire.[6]

A further example would be to see the real face of those people transpiring behind their apparent face, let alone with the makeup. You see that those castles, well, they may have been made of cardboard, but they were manifesting a reality in the world of imagination which has some value. You begin to see something deeper than the way things appear. Then you see that people seem to be manipulated by invisible threads, and you yourself used to be in that condition, too. As Christ said: they do not know what they do.[7] You are awake.

So, you see how life situations are the very best objects of meditation instead of the artificial themes that our traditional practices have presented us with. These are the new perspectives of meditation for the future.

---

6 Inayat Khan, "Philosophy," in "Supplementary Papers," unpublished.
7 Luke 23:34.

Chapter 3

The Clue Is Beauty

When you begin a retreat, your thoughts are no longer being monitored by the kind of activities that we have to perform in everyday life, like clocking in for your job, arranging child care, paying the insurance on your car, or listening to the latest news. The consequence is that your mind tends to dawdle randomly. What is more, your emotions start surfacing with great force, to such an extent that you might become overwhelmed by them. You seek in retreat to find peace in yourself, and you realize you cannot reach this goal through the use of your personal will. We will need to explore this a little further before we go any deeper into the retreat process.

We try to arrive at a little clarity about our thinking, not by stifling our thinking but by watching how it is working. Do not be worried if your thoughts are random. We want to try to give them a direction rather than controlling them. That is the way to be creative. Remember that all creativity begins with what Prigogine calls a "fluctuation from the state of equilibrium."[1] Randomness is the way in which one state of orderli-

1 Ilya Prigogine (1917–2003) was a Belgian scientist, awarded the Nobel Prize in Chemistry in 1977.

ness is broken down so it can be replaced by a new one. Do not be afraid of the randomness of your thoughts.

You might tend to think, "I cannot meditate because my thoughts are random." The way of dealing with this is to be enthused. If you are watching a wonderful TV show and your cat comes into the room, you may be aware of your cat but you probably will not look at your cat. This would be a guideline for meditating. Let those random thoughts circulate in the twilight of your consciousness, but resist the temptation to let the spotlight of your consciousness keep wandering. Otherwise, your energy gets dissipated.

Let us always be very clear about our objective: our objective is awakening, realization, illumination, unfurling our being, being quickened by a new energy. This is not achieved by stifling your mind and forcing it to concentrate on an object or even contemplate that object. Meanwhile, there are all these emotions stirring in you that could cause real dismay. You know there are thoughts that are too painful to countenance, and accordingly we bury them in the unconscious. There they fester and cause a more permanent wound, which gradually deepens and gets worse. We do not realize how it affects our personality by making us bitter and sardonic.

It is not a good idea to just bypass all of this and not take it into account. Let us face it and confront it. The way to heal a wound is to open up the dressing and clean it. Of course, it is painful; but it has to come to the surface, rather than being neglected because you cannot face it.

You need to be enthused and inspired in order to face your wounds, but just confronting them is not good enough. We are not thinking of therapy so much as transmutation of suffering into joy. It is not good to think simply of a cure, because that would be returning to where one was before; whereas, an illness or a wound is an opportunity of evolving. Find a door into another perspective. With the help of music, for example, we can sometimes be inspired and uplifted.

Rather than considering those wounds as negative handicaps, turn the tables on them and consider them as positive challenges in life that are going to strengthen your ability. A challenge is going to call upon you to marshal the resources in your being that have not yet manifested as they might. It is exactly what we were talking about earlier: looking at things from a different point of view than the point of view from which we had been looking at them up till now. The way that we have been considering the situation is a point of view but is not an absolute, and certainly is not the only possible point of view. So consider alternate points of view.

Perhaps you have been hurt because somebody humiliated you, or did something that damaged you psychologically or even in your actual situation in life. There may be pain because you have failed to live up to your standards or your ideal. Or, you have been disappointed in your assessment of yourself because you were not successful in an examination, or you were turned down for a job, or somebody whom you fancied turned you down. You felt that person did not think you were up to their expectations.

There is always that sense of validation that gets eroded and causes a very incipient kind of pain. It is always there, so we feel very precarious and vulnerable. It takes all that we have to validate our self-esteem enough to be able to make a go of our lives. We are always afraid that somebody will find out how inadequate we are. So we cover ourselves under masks, which can only lead toward a kind of dishonesty within us that we do not like to live with.

Perhaps that is a rather inadequate description of the situation in which a lot of us are. The first thing to realize is that you are not the only one. In fact, the stronger you are the more vulnerable you are. The more successful people may well be afraid that their records will be beaten by someone else; you can never be too cocksure about yourself. There again, you have complementarity. An extraordinarily positive clue about this is to be found in Murshid's teaching when he speaks about the aristocracy of the soul and the democracy of the ego.[2]

This is something that is going to arise in your retreat; your sense of self-esteem is very vulnerable. At least when on retreat you hope that you will be able to make it. Maybe in life people are so mean that it is very difficult to make a success of your life, but at least in meditation you hope to be successful. If you are not, then you feel that you have failed in your last resort. So it is very dangerous to have expectations about a retreat. But there is one saving grace: we are the Divine Being—maybe defiled, maybe distorted and limited, like the pyramid model mentioned earlier, but we need to acknowledge the divinity of our being. That is the saving grace.

It is true that these are just words, and when you go through the dark night of the soul you do not have anything on which to cleave. These words or the words of anybody who is trying to help you are of absolutely

2 Inayat Khan, *The Art of Being and Becoming*, 211.

no use whatsoever. In fact, that is the terror of the dark night: that nobody can help you, and all of those things onto which you are holding fail you. That is a time when there is as Saint John of the Cross said, "a very faint, flickering light."[3] Like, maybe, the light of a buoy in a storm at sea, in the fog and mist. Sometimes the wind blows the mist away so that you have just a glimpse of that flickering light, and then it goes. Then you have difficulty believing it was there.

That is the degree of despair that people can reach in the dark night of the soul, and do not think that this is just an aberrant case. The challenge of our lives includes both victory and despair. You have to go through a breakdown before you can reach a breakthrough. You must not be surprised if, not just circumstances in your life, but all your conceptions and all your self-esteem, and everything on to which you used at least to hold, falters and lets you down, abandons you. Then that flicker of light—that is just a metaphor, of course— would be, for an example, supposing that life makes sense but that you do not feel it; or, supposing there is beauty behind it all, but that you cannot see it. You tell yourself, "I would be losing the chance of my life if I were to discount that altogether." There is a kind of internal intuition that saves you from despair—that can, and hopefully will, save you from despair.

As a matter of fact, the whole test is to learn not to count upon others, or upon circumstances; to discover your own beauty hidden behind your self-denigration. There is a kind of self-organizing faculty that is there

---

3 John of the Cross, *The Dark Night of the Soul*, bk. 2, chap. 8. This Spanish poet and mystic (1542–91) was a friend of Teresa of Avila, and founded the Discalced Carmelites.

and, whether we believe it or not, it is trying to break through against our standing in its way. We are always standing in the way of our own well-being. That is why renunciation plays a part here: because, if we are incongruously standing in the way of our well-being, then by giving up our will something deeper, that is, this self-organizing faculty, can start coming through.

There is something totally irrational in the human mind, a kind of contradiction; something self-destructive which is accentuated in certain religions by what is called false humility—that is, priding yourself in your humility. The more you denigrate yourself the more you feel good. But you feel bad at the same time. There is a contradiction there.

We are learning to reconcile opposites: the aristocracy of the soul together with the democracy of the ego. To reconcile the two has to do with our way of thinking, that one can be both at the same time. Normally you think that you can only be one or the other. We are talking about a different mode of thinking that you learn to develop in meditation.

Of course, you see that it contradicts the logic that we have learned at school. We have learned the logic of "or" and now the discoveries of artificial intelligence have uncovered the logic of "and" instead.

How can we see goodness when we think of the incredible degree of suffering of people everywhere in the world? Well, there are little sparks, little events, that send you a message: looking into the eyes of a baby will remind you that there is beauty somewhere; listening to beautiful music—wherever there is a little beauty coming through. Somehow it does not speak to our mind; it touches a very deep point in us where there is a kind of unconscious recollection of a state prior to our incarnation. Whether you believe it or not, the fact is that it is there; and it acts as a kind of rope of hope, a kind of safety rope, that hoists us out of our despair.

When things happen in life which are tragic or cataclysmic—terrible things can, and do, happen to people—it seems like the whole program of the world has gone awry. That was one of the terrible plights of people in concentration camps: it was not just the terrible discomfort, but the thought that a human heart could have reached the point of hurting another person to that extent. How can you believe in God? It even goes beyond believing and not believing in God. When you reach that point you doubt that there is meaningfulness and beauty behind all this.

Remember the safety buoys, those little events that remind you that there is some meaning behind it and some beauty. Whenever they flicker in the darkness they are something to which you can cleave, desperately, and that can pull you out of the quagmire.

A retreat is the great test of finding your real self hidden behind all those evaluations that you make, and of which you are convinced. This would be a way of applying the doctrines of maya, like the physical world is not the way it appears. Well, that is very perfunctory. But that our picture of ourselves is maya—this goes much deeper. We must abandon any effort of trying to assess our value. Our minds, in their commonplace mode, find it difficult to reconcile the irreconcilables, and our efforts to validate ourselves are misleading unless we can reconcile the irreconcilables.

That is what we are learning to do. At first the mind does not see the logic of it because we are used to the logic of "or." Our thinking stands in the way. That is why in meditation you really are learning how to think from scratch. Our thinking was mistaken in the beginning and has led us from one point to another in a fall from a sublime state. That is why in our meditations we suggest working with something very concrete.

We are beginning to see how mind thinks. We are beginning to modulate it, to have some ability to modulate it, which is not the same thing as controlling. In controlling you are limiting, whereas here you are allowing it to alternate, and then collating or extrapolating between those two views. Deeper still is modulating emotion.

The thing that precipitates the despair is that our concept of God avers itself to be deceptive. Pir-o-Murshid points that out very clearly when he says that we tend to confuse our concept of God with our experience of God.[4] We are talking about God, but surreptitiously, unaware, we are thinking; and when we say "God" we mean our concept of God. We are confusing ourselves.

Pir-o-Murshid is saying that the concept can be like a scaffolding, but that you need to be able to destroy that. For example, you see the Tibetans building a beautiful mandala and then destroying the whole thing. It is very painful to see that beautiful thing destroyed, but the whole idea is to destroy the idol—just as in Islam. Our concepts of God are the idol, and can serve as a prop. But at a certain moment they are an obstacle. We see

4 *Vision of God and Man*, 31.

this enacted, in the great traditions of the world, when at Easter time the God is destroyed. The idol is destroyed, is burnt, and replaced by a new one.

Then you find yourself in that very deep place in the dark night. All that we have thought of and believed in proves to be nonsense, and we cannot replace it by anything, unless we make that step which Pir-o-Murshid describes as the experience of God. But then the immediate answer, the response, of the Sufis is that God can never be the object of your experience because God is the subject experiencing. Then you find yourself in this terrible quandary—unless your mind is trained.

That is why the more illuminated teachings, whatever the religion, will give us some kind of clues. Here we refer to Sufism, because Sufism is concerned with the experience of God rather than the concept of God. There is no dogma, it is purely experience. But if you talk about experience you are talking about a subject and an object, and we have already seen that is deceptive. The kind of experience or the kind of realization that we come to through that is deceptive. We have to know how we can modulate experience so that the experience of God becomes a reality.

These will serve as principles for retreat. As you are sitting there meditating, you are aware of the physical world. You want to include the physical world in your awareness but a modified perspective of it. The physical world seems to be a little remote, like that cat that enters your room when you are looking at TV; a little remote, but you do not cut it out altogether.

Instead of saying this is all maya, the first theme in your meditation is to think something is trying to transpire behind that which appears. It is not God exactly; but it is what the Sufis call *ayat*: signs, or clues. These are the spores of the Divine Being. They are like the pugmarks of a bear in the snow; you have not seen the bear, but they give you some clue.

God can never be the object of your knowledge, but there are some signs: namely, wherever you see beauty. In your despair, beauty is the clue if you can see it transpire. And actually, it is to be seen everywhere; but one has to have the eyes to see it. For an example, the photons in a beer can on a garbage heap are as beautiful as the photons of the stars. It is a question of seeing it.

A more concrete way of doing this is to see the beauty in the faces of people behind the masks that they are wearing; and even the beauty of your own face looking in the mirror, if you can see what transpires instead of that which appears. Ascribe what you do not like about what you see to the fact that we have had to borrow the fabric of our ancestors, and that we have been subjected to stress and pain and deception. It is true that the outer aspect of our being has suffered from distortion and defilement, but we have to look deeper.

That is the first principle in a retreat: that you are always on the lookout for that which transpires behind that which appears. If you are walking in the snow, something transpires through that scene, a kind of immaculate condition. If you were to look at the crystals of snow you would realize how very beautiful they are, that the symmetrical shape of the crystal configures meaningfulness in the universe. It is unmistakable that there is meaningfulness there, otherwise they would all be random. You have found a clue.

Suppose you are talking to a person and there is something about that person that you do not like. Often, if there is something in a person that you dislike, it is because you have the same thing in yourself. Speaking with that person causes you to like yourself even less. But try to see if you can detect some beauty in that person. Maybe you do not want to see it because, again, it is so challenging to your mind. You cannot reconcile it with all the bad you see. But that is the first step, that which transpires. Remember this principle: always look for that which transpires behind that which appears.

You could carry it further and watch for that which transpires behind situations, especially ugly situations. Something is coming through. It is sometimes very difficult to see. It can come through surprisingly. For example, what happened in the Soviet Union: that, somehow, the need for freedom managed to overcome all the resistance.[5] There was beauty there that was grasping for expression. Our whole outer construct can break down facing the quest for beauty.

These are the things to look for: beauty or meaningfulness. They are two aspects of the same thing. The scientists call it elegance. First of all, you look at the physical world; then you look at situations where you see beauty. For an example, you may have heard of that catastrophe in which a plane landed in the water in Washington, D.C., and you think of the horror of it. But then you think of that man who kept on offering other people to come before him. There is beauty there. There is beauty in the donkey upon which Christ rode. There is beauty in the downtrodden, not just the victorious—perhaps even more beauty, because there is no

5 The dissolution of the Soviet Union occurred in 1991.

show. It is real; there is no pretense. It is not that which glitters that is beautiful.

The next thing is to discover God, not through the signs outside, but through the signs inside your personality. They are trying to come through. You apply the same principle: that which transpires, or is trying to transpire, behind that which appears. What appears may be a distortion of it. For example, mastery may manifest as being on an ego trip; or peacefulness may manifest as laziness, or slovenliness, or indolence; and joy may manifest as frivolity or facetiousness.

So, instead of judging yourself by what appears in your personality—perhaps there are things that you do not like—remember that behind them there is something beautiful that is trying to come through. The person on an ego trip is trying to develop mastery, and the facetious person is trying to give vent to joy, and so on. God is trying to come through, or, let us say, the divine nature is trying to come through. What appears at first is a veil, as the Sufis would say. See this in yourself.

Once more: this is a theme of meditation. Instead of concentrating on an object and trying to control your mind, discover that which is trying to come through you. You see that it gets distorted by losing the connection with what you might call the being of God, with the totality. Being encapsulated within your personal self-image—that is where it gets distorted. Continually remind yourself that the whole universe is the manifestation of God and the actuation of God. This means looking at things from a much wider perspective. And, it is happening in you. These are the Sufi meditations.

Using this model, you discover God by creating God as your being, by actuating God as your being.

It is a knowledge that is acquired by doing. Instead of thinking of yourself as the instrument through which God manifests, or actuates the Divine Being, think of yourself as the being of God that has become focalized—limited in a funnel, as it were. Just as, if you take the water from the ocean and put it in a jug, it is still the water of the ocean. Do not think of it merely as limited, but also distorted as, for example, the voice of Caruso was distorted by the bad recordings of the time. It still is the voice of Caruso, but distorted. So, think of yourself as the being of God, but there is some distortion that has taken place. The pristine state remains unscathed within its distortion.

You are afraid that your love will be misconstrued. You are afraid that your compassion will invite people to abuse it, that your joy will hurt the feelings of pain of the person with whom you speak, that your mastery will reinforce your ego. There are reasons because of which it is difficult to unfurl the potentialities of your being, the divine qualities that you are. It is necessary, then, to be very clear about what is holding you back, where the obstacles are to those qualities being enhanced so that you may become a beautiful person in a beautiful world. You have to do work with yourself in order to remove those obstacles. That is the thing to do in a retreat.

For example, if you are able to cleanse your love so that it becomes unconditional love, then the chances are that people will not misconstrue it. If you see the difference between generosity and permissiveness you find that in Kabbalah, the association of Chesed and Gevurah, both together—compassion, or generosity, and, at the same time, severity—then you are better able to reconcile these two, and you are better able to have compassion without it being abused.

Or, for example, being truthful: you do not have to be critical of people in their face to be truthful. It is a matter of being truthful in your being, authentic in your being. Your authenticity will cause the persons with whom you have contact to become aware of the failings for which you would otherwise have criticized them.

We are removing obstacles in our thinking. These are obstacles standing in the way of our unfolding the potentialities that are lying in wait in our being. They will continue merely to lie in wait unless we remove the obstacles.

Consider peacefulness, for example: you do not have to lie on the beach munching chocolate to be peaceful. You can be peaceful in the middle of a very hectic life. Or, freedom: find an inner freedom and then, however constraining the circumstances are, it will not take anything away from your internal freedom. In fact, the more free you are inside the more you can involve yourself with situations and with people in a way that does not rob them of their freedom and will not rob you of your own freedom.

This is really the way that God, or the divine nature, comes through your personality. The signs of that nature are there, latent within you, and trying to come through. It is only as it comes through that the divine nature can become known to you. There is no use saying "I need to know what my divine inheritance is before I can actuate it." It is the other way around: you need to actuate it in order to discover it.

By discovering the divine nature trying to come through your personality, you feel that you are closer to

what is understood by "the being of God" than you are
by gathering clues observing the physical world. There
are two further steps at which you feel a still greater
closeness.

You normally think that you are the observer, observing
the physical world or observing the situation or person, or even observing your thought or your psyche. That
would be the general, commonplace state in which
most people are. The next step—this is again a practice
to do while on retreat—would be to consider yourself to
be the instrument through which God sees. Your eyes
are the lenses through which the divine glance looks
into the universe. That is a wonderful way of looking
at things in a meditation retreat. Your glance is like the
two windows through which God looks into the universe.

Of course, it is not satisfactory because you are still
thinking in terms of duality. In orthodox religion, you
will find what Professor Gershom Scholem termed an
exaggerated sense of the otherness of God[6]—whereas
in the mystical approach, you see the unity—and it
would be a mistake to think of yourself as the instrument through which God sees. That leads to the next
stage: considering your glance as an extension of the
divine glance, which is focalized and thereby funneled
down and limited.

Now return to the theme, and consider your problems
as being the object of your meditation. Instead of considering them from a personal vantage point, consider
that your insight, or your understanding, is an extension
of the divine understanding that has been focalized,

---

6 Gershom Scholem (1897–1982) founded a school in which
the rigorous study of Jewish mysticism transformed the study of
Kabbalah. See his *Major Trends in Jewish Mysticism*.

funneled down, limited. You see now that your problems are going to look very different from the way they look when you think of yourself as a spectator considering them.

The immediate question is, how can we know what the point of view of God would be? The answer is to be found in the words of Henri Poincaré, a great mathematician, who said that we have an inherent ability to grasp infinity that consists in, for example, always being able to imagine a larger number than any number that one can imagine.[7] We know that however great we imagine a number, there is always a greater number. So somehow our ability to embrace infinity, to reach out toward infinity in infinite regress, is written right into our latent potentialities.

That is why we can imagine what the perfection of a human quality would be, for example, compassion; we can imagine what the divine compassion could be. We have that ability. In fact, it is that ability which helps us to reach beyond our limitations. The divine compassion is present within our limited compassion, just like the voice of Caruso is present within its distortion.

In the same way, we have the ability to imagine how things would look from the divine point of view, provided that we understand that it is in infinite regress. In other words, we understand that we can never attain it totally.

We also have the ability to develop a greater insight into things than the insight that we have developed so far.

---

7 Henri Poincaré, *Science and Hypothesis*, 17 and following. Poincaré (1854–1912) was a French mathematician and scientist, well known for his efforts to explain science to the public.

Instead of imagining that you are the eyes through which God sees, think that you are the divine glance that has become funneled and, therefore, focalized, and therefore, limited. But it still is the divine glance; it is not another glance. Think of the glance as being active, rather than thinking in terms of reacting to an impression or receiving an impression. That is the whole idea of the lamp of Aladdin: it is like a torch that illuminates like a spotlight, a beam that illuminates things.[8]

There are a few clues in Murshid's teaching that will be helpful here. For example, seeing beyond the sight of the eyes, or understanding beyond the grasp of the mind. Or then: the eyes see what they are able to see but the soul sees beyond what the eyes can see.[9] The ability of the soul to see—that may seem like metaphor, but if you have done astral travel, or have had out-of-body experience, then you realize that, indeed, it is true that you can see without eyes.

Now let us just backtrack a little bit. Ibn 'Arabi poses the question: How can one know God, as God can never be the object of your knowledge?[10] Ibn 'Arabi said you only know the archetype through the exemplar. You never know the archetype itself. If you think of the qualities that we named, the names, and you consider that they are archetypes, obviously they are not knowable except in their exemplars—that is, in your personality or in

8 Inayat Khan, *Mastery through Accomplishment*, 104.
9 *In An Eastern Rose Garden*, vol. 7, *The Sufi Mesage of Hazrat Inayat Khan*, 43.
10 Muhyi ad-Din Ibn 'Arabi (1165–1240) is widely regarded as the foremost proponent of Sufi metaphysics. He has been called "the red sulfur," an alchemical reference implying that Ibn 'Arabi could draw knowledge out of ignorance just as sulfur draws gold out of lead.

the personalities of other people. That is where you can see them. You only know roundness by experiencing round objects. Do not think that you can grasp the archetypes in themselves. God can never be the object of your knowledge.

As we got into being the divine glance, we got closer to what we mean by God, because God cannot be thought of as an object—only as a subject. That is where we get closer to what we mean by God. But there is a further step. However much you think that your glance is the divine glance that has become funneled and limited, according to Shabistari it is only the reflection of the divine glance. We refer to his words because they are very important, but we are also translating them into modern concepts. The physical world is a hologram. A hologram is not maya, it is a real construct of light; but it is only a replicate of the image behind it and that image can never be the object of your knowledge. But it does give you a clue as to the nature of the image behind it.[11]

This is, of course, a metaphor, an illustration. In reality, in the instance of the world, the image behind the hologram does not have a form. It acquires a form when it has been projected. Since it is not a form, it can never be the object of your knowledge.

In the same way, your consciousness is a reflection, a projection, of the divine consciousness. So, we thought we got there when we imagined we were an extension

---

11 Mahmud Shabistari, *The Secret Rose Garden*, 46–53. Shabistari (d. 1320) lived in Tabriz in Azerbaijan in Iran. The main focus of *The Secret Rose Garden* (*Gulshan-i raz*) is the unity of being and the perfect human being, the central concepts of Sufi theory after the time of Ibn 'Arabi.

of the divine glance; but there is always something beyond it. That is where we move into transcendence, because, of course, we cannot limit God to the divine immanence. As we said in our invocation: God who outstrips any concept that we could possibly make of God.

That is why al-Hallaj said: "How do you think that you can confer upon God a mode of knowing? In one stroke of his transcendental knowledge he can shatter any knowledge that you think you have, and replace it with a whiff of his understanding that you can never hold. It will dissolve before you have thought you have experienced it." These are the words of al-Hallaj.[12]

There is a still deeper experience of God, beyond all that we have been talking about; and that is the divine presence. It is not limited by the qualities; it is not predicated by the qualities. Therefore, the names will not convey it. The zikr will.[13] If we are saying that a person is present we are not predicating anything about the nature of that person. The only thing to clarify is your concept of presence. We generally think of the divine presence as other than ourselves, and the ultimate realization comes when you discover that you are that presence. That is the ultimate secret, and that is a clue to the power of the dervish.

---

12 Husayn ibn Mansur Hallaj (857–922) was, and continues to be, a controversial figure; he was crucified after being convicted of heresy, and is famous for having said, "Ana al-Haqq" (I am the Truth). He is the prototypical ecstatic, whose utterances and descriptions in poetry of his mystical experience have been a paradox through the centuries. His life and teachings can be studied in detail in Louis Massignon's *The Passion of al-Hallaj*.

13 Zikr is the cardinal practice of the Sufis. The practice includes chanting or repetition of the phrase *La ilaha illa 'Llab hu*, which declares both the unity and the presence of God.

When you have grasped that you are the divine presence, then, according to the Sufis, you observe, or exhibit, the manner of God, *akhlaq Allah*. You do things with great nobility, and you are endowed with a divine power, and, more than ever, you convey divine emotion.

There is nothing more shattering and transforming than divine emotion. It is far beyond the personal emotions: joy and pain, delight and anger. You are continually being pummeled by your personal emotions, but in the realization of the divine presence the emotion is sublime, divine, uplifting. It manifests through your personal emotions which have become noble and beautiful. Buddha phrased this in very clear terms: your degree of realization will translate itself in terms of decorum, which is probably the same word as excellence. The pursuit of excellence is the final goal, the final objective. Do not think it is utopic or beyond reach; it is always good to have a clear objective and then move toward it. The pull of the future is stronger than the push of the past.

Chapter 4

Dealing with Impressions

In meditation, you will find that it is the observation of your breath that monitors its rhythm. Simply observing the breath will tend to slow it down.

The breath can act as a swing; so, as you exhale you could think of radiating, and as you inhale you could think of being veiled. The Sufis have the word *zahir* for radiating; think of a star or, rather, the whole world as the epiphany, the manifestation of the nonmanifest. And, as you inhale, we have the word *batin*, which means "the veiled one," referring to those aspects of yourself that have not yet manifested to view—the potentialities of your being.

It also means, of course, the many-splendored potentialities of the universe that are trying to come through but have not yet manifested to view. Your resourcefulness, your potentialities, are part of all in the universe that has not yet manifested to view and is continually trying to come through.

As you exhale, you experience the way that certain qualities are trying to come through your personality. They manifest as your personality. So you are oscillating, or alternating, your consciousness and your attunement on the swing of the breath. The breath acts as a swing.

The more peaceful you are, the more your breath will slow down. In a retreat you invert the usual attitude, so that you are not trying to achieve anything or prove yourself to yourself. Consequently, you can reverse the machine that is usually so hyperactive and find peace. Your breathing is going to be slower, and you can go much more deeply into this oscillation between manifesting and withdrawing into the depth of your being, which is not yet manifest. You begin to feel something about the potentialities or hidden faculties that you have not developed so far.

As you exhale, you realize that there are no boundaries to your life-field or to your aura. You are like a vortex, which does not have a boundary; but it is very difficult to reconcile this with the fact that you do have a boundary. If it were not so, you would not have a choice between those elements from the environment that you want to ingest and those which you want to repel. Everyone would be like everybody else; there would be no selectivity at all. It is the ability to select among impressions those that we want to incorporate in our being that makes for the splendid variety of human beings, and even animals, at the individual scale. When you inhale, think that your life-field is constituted of zones, protective zones. You could think of them as thresholds. You consider that the impressions from the environment get filtered—not just once, but there are several filters, several zones—until you reach inside, which is the immaculate state, and which can never be tarnished by the impressions.

At the surface of your being there is a spillover from the environment, so it is true that at that edge you are like a vortex without a boundary. But you get more and more a sense of your individual idiosyncrasies as you breathe in, as you draw closer and closer to the center. That is the first thing you do. These are the steps leading to samadhi.

If you are sitting in meditation, you are not experiencing the physical world. Your eyes are closed, you are not paying attention to the sound of the cars in the street and all the commotion around, the TV sets and so on. You are in a very different state.

The physical world continues to live in you in the form of impressions. We are living in a world in which some of those impressions are very gross, disturbing, and destructive; so if you are simply delivered into the hands of the impressions from outside you get very badly shredded at the jagged ends of your being. You lose your attunement and your individuality, your individualness.

This is where your scale of values will help you to determine which are the impressions that you want to allow very deeply into your psyche and which are those you find destructive or harmful. There is a criterion, and the criterion is: those impressions that are in resonance with your being and those that are too foreign to it. That is the principle upon which the immune system is built: me or not me. You would see this, for example, when receiving an organ transplant: if it is very similar, if the code of the DNA is very similar to that of your own body, then you can incorporate it more easily.

There are methods of forcing the body to accept an organ that does not really belong to it. And it is true that the body has the ability to adapt itself to elements that are foreign to it, otherwise you would not be able to eat. But this ability tends to become overstressed in our society. Consequently, you lose your specific nature, and then you start disliking yourself because you are not living up to your ideals. It is your scale of values that determines which are the elements that you incorporate and which are those that you reject.

This is something you can do very consciously, because, as you are meditating, impressions will hit your consciousness. In the psyche, there is a whole structure of defense systems. An impression may break through quite a number of defense systems and reach into a very vulnerable place in your psyche. Then it becomes endemic and obsessive. It is very difficult to get rid of those impressions that are then part of your psyche.

It is a matter of the balance between the degree to which you adapt yourself to the environment and the degree to which you adapt the environment to your own sense of purpose. If you want to fulfill your purpose in life you need to be creative, and that means to work upon the environment rather than allow yourself to be totally submerged in the environment. The practice of the zikr is very helpful, because you are generating centrifugal forces that have the effect of repelling impressions that are not wanted.

In a retreat you can see this very clearly. Of course, some of the impressions are already there; they have already gained entry into your psyche. So, you could exert yourself, as you inhale, to repel any new impressions that are harmful. Those impressions are repelled from outside, as it were; they never gain entry. And, as you exhale, you could drain damaging impressions from the environment that are already in you, just like the immune system, through the operation of the lymph glands, drains toxins from the body.

You are repelling the impressions that are trying to come through, to gain entrance, by the centrifugal forces of your being. Buddha calls it placing a sentinel at the doors of perception. You can do that by being very aware of who you are, affirming who you are. You have to be truly uncompromising in order to really be who you are, otherwise you are just anybody or everybody. You can see the difference between that, repelling impressions that are other than you and then draining toxins, psychological toxins, that are causing harm within you—draining them downward. There you have two directions of breath: one is centripetal/centrifugal, the other is ascending/descending. So try to become aware of those two different ways of dealing with impressions that are unwanted.

For each person there are certain values: the scale of values of one person is not the same as another's. You have to be true to your scale of values. There are two forces that are at work here, that are operative. One could be translated in the divine name *haqq*, which means the "truth"; and the other in the name *quddus*, which means "pure spirit."

It is your dedication to the truth which will prove uncompromising, and therefore will repel, will keep out, elements that are harmful. Working with the centripetal/centrifugal forces gives you strength. As you exhale, you reinforce your defense system, which is, for example, repelling memories from the environment that are harmful, by the power of truth. You do this as you exhale, by the power of truth.

Now you introduce retention of breath between inhaling and exhaling. This is a new factor. As you hold your breath, you find yourself in the internal condition. You have turned inward; the whole universe is to be found inside. You reach out into the universe from inside; we have already studied that. Now we want to highlight one aspect of the many aspects of that internal state, the implicate state, and that is the purity of it. Think of the words of Pir-o-Murshid: the core of your being is like a mirror that can never be tarnished by the impressions upon it.[1] It has its own immunity. That is the meaning of *quddus*—pure spirit.

Still, those harmful impressions can get very close to the core of your being and enshroud it or becloud it. So think of purity as being a kind of pervasive force that gradually gains ground, such that the core of your being becomes wider and wider by pushing away those elements that are polluted. It is like cleansing from within. It is your concern about purity that does not brook of pollution, rather than the power of *haqq*, the power of truth. You are not using force so much as honoring your ideal.

As you exhale, you do have a sense of being boundless, of expansion. The divine name for expansion is *basit*. You do not seem to have a boundary. When you inhale, you draw your attention to the boundaries, the protective boundaries. You are both, and it is very difficult to reconcile these irreconcilables in your mind: that you are both boundless and yet do have boundaries.

The second approach to working with impressions is distilling the impressions that would normally be

1 *Healing and the Mind World*, vol. 4, *The Sufi Message of Hazrat Inayat Khan*, 197.

indigestible. That is what the body does with food. The impressions are broken down and rebuilt again. If you were to isolate yourself from everything that is not yourself, you would be inbred in your being; you would never be enriched by the interface with the universe.

The way to do this is exactly what the body does with its food—to transmute the impressions that are not in resonance with your being. The more evolved a person is the more that you can encompass things that are not in harmony with your being. The consequence is that you can love people of whom you are very critical; this is not expansion, but encompassing. As you expand, you become more encompassing. You have the sense of immensity plus the sense of having a boundary; but the boundary is extremely vast. The name for that is *wasi*.

If you do this you will realize that a lot of people live in your being, in your consciousness. They are always present, and it can be painful. The metaphor that we find in the East is that you become like an oyster that has a grit of sand in its body. You transform the grit of sand into a pearl, and then it becomes more acceptable. That is *wasi*.

That is also the meaning of *rahman*: to have room in your heart for people who are obnoxious or who make themselves difficult to love. When you can find that room in your heart, then you become a great being. That is *rahman*.

Be careful about the notion of boundaries to your being, because you are as small or as great as the boundaries that you set for your being. And we want to unmask a myth: however much you expand you could never lose yourself, although you might think you have lost yourself. There are people who want to lose themselves because they do not like themselves. They go into samadhi, yet they never succeed in losing themselves, because you cannot even if you try. It is just like an eddy on the surface of a lake: you have lost sight of it, you think it is gone. But it is only caught up in a wave interference pattern. It still can be retrieved. That is a good thought.

It is very dangerous to seek to lose yourself. You can get yourself to believe, you can deceive yourself into thinking that you have lost yourself. There is even a kind of pride in losing yourself. But remember the words of the Sufis: "It is out of love for you that I descended from the solitude of unity." So it would be most ungrateful to God to wish to destroy the very purpose that God was seeking in you.

We have been working with the periphery of our being. Now we are going to move toward the center. And we discover an extraordinary thing: elements of the environment that have passed, have broken through, the defenses and got very close to the center can be eliminated by resorbing them in the void inside you. The center of a vortex is a void. This is something you experience when you hold your breath after inhaling.

Think of a void. A very good metaphor is Buddha sitting in the middle of a storm, yet where he sat it was perfectly peaceful. He was sitting in the center of the storm, which is a vacuum. It is a good thought. You can think of your life as full of turmoil, strife all over the place. Yet you are sitting there in a peaceful state in the middle of all that turbulence. You have touched upon the vacuum where everything is resorbed. Just like the sea will absorb the pollution we inflict upon it up to a point, the vacuum inside you is kind enough to resorb some degree of pollution.

It is not the impressions from outside which are being resorbed here. It is those impressions that have become so much a part of your being that you cannot even consider them as impressions anymore. You might like to think that there is a purification process taking place here, and that you are continually being recycled, which is true. For example, every wave is introjected back into the sea, and it is the whole sea that emerges as every new wave.

But there is another way of looking at it: that you are continually, recurrently, reborn anew. That is a much better way of countering those aspects in your being that you dislike; that is, by replacing them with something positive. This is where creativity makes all the difference, and that again has to do with your thinking. You need to accept that you can be a totally new person, instead of thinking that you have to keep on schlepping your old being into the future.

Concentrate on that. After inhaling, hold your breath, and, at the moment when you are transiting between holding the breath and exhaling, feel as though a new dispensation has emerged out of the void—ex nihilo, out of the void— and that you are a new person.

We do not enrich ourselves only by our interfacing with the universe, but by creativity—the self-organizing creativity that emerges from within. That balance is very important, particularly for a creative person. Are you simply processing the impressions you have received from outside? In a musical composition, for example, if you are a composer, are you simply reverberating that which you have picked up from the environment or is it totally new? The fact is that the impressions from outside act as catalysts that are going to call forth a new dispensation emerging from the depths of your being. Otherwise we are not creative; we are simply reacting instead of acting.

You see all the way you have come from where you started off: you were alternating between being conscious of the environment and turning within, you were toggling between the two. Then, at a certain point, you began to see a correspondence; for example, that you saw yourself in another person, and the other person in yourself. There is a correspondence between the inner and the outer. We have to see ourselves in other ourselves to be better able to manifest what we are.

You have moved from there into adding to the interface with the environment a new factor: that which is emerging from inside. Now, how do you do it?

It is helpful that while you are meditating you not place a wall between the environment and yourself, which would encapsulate you in your psyche. Still, you have been placing sentinels that filter through the impressions. And you could bring about a situation in which you do block out the environment for a short while—if for nothing else, then because you can get to a point when you have an indigestion of impressions from outside, and you need to give yourself time to digest it all. But that is only one reason.

The other reason to do this, to block out the environment, is that when the sun is in the sky you cannot see the stars. It is very difficult to become cognizant of all the wealth inside if you are still preoccupied with the way things look in the explicate condition. It is, as Pir-o-Murshid said, like taking the mirror that is normally turned toward the physical world, toward perception and also expression, and turning it the opposite direction.[2] That is where you find this metaphor of the veiled one. You are not just surrounded by zones, with sentinels filtering perceptions, but now you are really putting a blind on the environment for a time. Remember, though, that this is a practice to do only while on retreat.

You could do this with your will, but it would be harmful. You have to do it with your emotions. The word used in the East is *vairagya*, indifference toward outer conditions. We understand that it has very serious consequences in terms of the material life, but you must be able to do it for a short while, and particularly in a retreat situation.

You are withdrawing your interest from the ambient circumstances: physical, social, and environmental. You are not taking in impressions from the outside world anymore, so that you are open to intuition—that is, impressions which emerge from within.

Usually, as you inhale you are absorbing impressions from the outside world, and as you exhale you are radiating them. In a sense, from your usual perspective, your breath operates the holomovement, to use David Bohm's term, between the external and the internal, the explicate and the implicate. Now we are going to have to adopt a whole new way of thinking about breath: do not consider it anymore as a metronome that determines your alternating between the external world and the internal.

How do you do that? Well, by holding your breath, by marking a pause between inhaling and exhaling; be-

2 Inayat Khan, *The Awakening of the Human Spirit*, 144–45.

cause your inbreath and outbreath act as a metronome. When you slow it down, you slow your sense of the rhythm of the process of becoming. But if you interrupt your breath altogether, you have lost your sense of time.

When we talk about breath, we mean what the Hindus call *prana*, which is energy, the pulsing of energy. This is a word that has meaning in science. For example, waves are not waves of air, but waves of energy. When we think of energy, think of the magnetic field or even of light. Those are the manifestations of energy, but they are not energy. They are the manifestations of energy, just like a wave could be a wave of a wheat field or a grass field. It is not the grass that is the wave. The wave is a wave of energy.

If you think this way, then you do not think of breath anymore as the energy that moves the stars, but something much more profound. It is very difficult to describe, but this is the method that you could use: after inhaling, as you hold your breath, you could imagine that the oxygen, for example, continues to pervade your body by moving into the arteries and, eventually, into the cells of your body. That gives you the impression of what is meant in esoteric law by internal energy instead of external energy.

This is just one method. It is helpful not to limit your breath to inhaling and exhaling, but to think of the way that energy percolates in your body. This could be just a metaphor, but still we want to go deeper— that is, instead of breathing with your body, if we may say it this way, breathing with your soul.

There are Sufi practices that will help you to reach that very subtle sense of what we mean by *quddus*, the energy of pure spirit. First, you want to distinguish between four forces. Try and see if you can experience these forces.

To begin, imagine that you are sitting in nature surrounded by beautiful greenery and basking in the sun. You are feeling all this energy around you. You are absorbing this energy as you inhale and it is giving you a lot of vitality, tangible vitality. Your body is strengthened by it as you inhale. And, as you exhale, you think that where you are sitting the flowers begin to blossom. You are communicating life to everything around you.

This kind of energy is what we call *hayy*. You get to a point when that is something very important to do: to feel that wherever you go you communicate life. You know that wonderful poem: wherever you go, the blushing flowers shall arise and all things shall flourish.[3] You are communicating life to the people you meet, to the flowers, to the animals.

That is the kind of energy that you will increase by thinking of the way in which your magnetic field converges the magnetic field of the cosmos. Also, consider how your magnetic field expands and dynamizes the environment. You can even feel such an incredible expanse of magnetism, a zone of magnetism, around your body that you find it difficult to pass through a doorway. People will feel it and will be drawn to you because you will be a source of energy. That is what people need most, much more than understanding: life energy.

If you hold your breath between inhaling and exhaling, and you shift into the internal state, then you will

3 This line is from an aria in Handel's *Semele*, "Where'er You Walk."

discover a new dispensation of energy that arises from the void. This energy regenerates, not only your body, but everything around you. And the word for that is *muhyi*. You will also discover another force, which is always present in some way when *muhyi* is active, and that is *mu'id*: resilience, the ability of all things to return to the condition in which they were before they had been disturbed.

The branch of the tree will return to its position if you disturb it. If you disturb the rain forests, they will grow again. That is therapy. Therapy is based upon getting back to your original healthy condition. But muhyi represents the ability to be better, after having been ill, than you were before you were ill. In other words, to regenerate, to evolve, to improve. It is not static. *Mu'id* is static, whereas *muhyi* is dynamic. Of course, there has to be balance between the two, or else the forces of regeneration would run amok. There has to be some balance.

That is what you experience as you hold your breath. You will find that you grasp the new energy at the moment when you transit between holding your breath and exhaling. That is when you feel *muhyi*, the power of regeneration. You feel *mu'id* when you are transiting between the inhaling and the holding of the breath.

Then we have a fourth force, which we call *quddus*, and which seems to descend upon you instead of emerging from the depth. It has a shattering power; it shatters you. It shatters all the status quo and triggers off *muhyi* and *hayy*. It quickens.

When you are doing your breathing practices, it is important to recognize each of these four forces.

After breathing in and before breathing out, follow your breath by internalizing it. Imagine that your soul is breathing in and out instead of your body, while you are holding your physical breath. You are suspending your physical breath. You are getting in touch with the real energy that moves the universe.

The energy that moves the universe is not the one that you can tap or even ascertain by measuring the energy experienced in the physical world. It is a kind of internal energy which reaches outward to manifest in the physical world. It is a totally different kind of energy. Pir-o-Murshid says that you get in touch with the hidden mechanism behind everything that manifests at the surface.[4]

When you look at your life you could see it as though it is moving from inside toward the surface, toward outside. We have already said this, but this brings it all much more into focus: the light of your aura is simply the manifestation of the light that you are. So, instead of thinking that is the reality—the light of your aura—understand that the real light is the light that sees rather than the light that can be seen. If you think this way, you can continually arouse the deep springheads of your being to the manifested state. The potentialities of your being will become visible, audible, tangible, and knowable.

Perhaps the strongest experience here is emotion. Your deep emotion arises just like the waves arise out of the depth of the sea. Your emotion acquires a very great power. It moves the souls of humans. It is not joy, and it is not the pain you are suffering: these continue at the surface. But behind the personal emotions, emerg-

4 *The Alchemy of Happiness*, vol. 6, *The Sufi Message of Hazrat Inayat Khan*, 168.

ing from the depth of your being is a kind of cosmic emotion. Maybe it is *'ishq Allah*, the divine nostalgia. You feel so moved by the meaning of life, the meaning of yourself in life, the meaning of people in life—what it is all about, what comes to view, what comes to the surface and how, and what it means.

You see that this is quite a different matter than thinking that you are converging the physical universe. You are working internally. Think of the words of Jalal ad-Din Rumi: "If I could only express what moves my soul, the world would be flooded by the power of its emotion." This thought links you with the very foundation of your being, the rockbed of your being. Then, when you find yourself facing problems and conditions, you are able to avail yourself of the power of this emotion. It will make all the difference in the way that you handle problems and situations. You would not be acting from the surface of your being, but from the depth.

If you shut the shutters of your soul to the outer world, then your consciousness has no choice but to seek to experience within. Do not let yourself be deceived by the thoughts and emotions of your personal psyche, because that represents a relatively superficial level of your being. We are talking about a much deeper level than the level that is generally called the psyche, or the unconscious, and which psychotherapists are trying to touch upon. That level of thought is the result of something deeper. Your psyche is the expression of something much deeper. You are not really getting down to the core of your being by exploring your personal psyche. The deeper roots are more and more impersonal. Think of your psyche as a projection of your real being.

Chapter 5

Zikr

If you are familiar with Sufi practices you may have already recognized that the things that we have been considering in the preceding chapters are embodied in the practice of the zikr. Begin the practice by whirling your head: moving from your left shoulder, down to your left knee, across to your right knee, up to your right shoulder, and back to the zenith. Imagine that you are tracing with your third eye a circle of light. Even your heart is forming a circle of light. But if you become aware of your crown center at the top of your head, then you will seem to be tracing a spiral that gets increasingly large as you whirl, and reaches right into the stars.

As you do this, especially if you get into the feeling of the spiral, you will feel the centrifugal forces. And, keeping with what we have said, there are two aspects of it: one is the expansion of your being, and the counterpart is the repelling of the impressions of the environment that you do not wish to ingest—both at the same time. You are highlighting the periphery of your being, of your psyche, and even of your body—where there is a spillover from the environment, between you and the environment.

Consider that aspect of your psyche that you call your psyche—that you think you own your thoughts, for example—as being right out there at the periphery. It is superficial; it is not the depth of your being. It is continually co-mingling with the environment, the psychological environment, and it is gradually getting dissolved and renewed. For the moment you are thinking of it being dissolved.

The center around which you gravitate, you whirl, is your solar plexus. Instead of thinking that your physical body is whirling, you could identify with your magnetic field. So, you are churning the magnetic field of the environment with your magnetic field. Then you could consider that it is your aura that is whirling. Instead of it just being a circle of light, it is sparkling with light— just like in those statues of Nataraja, Shiva is sparkling with light all around.

You are strongly aware of the fact that you are circumambulating a center. You know that circumambulating a center is going to strengthen your concentration on the center. While you are right out there toward the periphery, you feel the suction effect of the vacuum at the center—as we said, the vacuum at the center of a vortex. You access that center through your solar plexus. That center is immobile and silent, whereas the circle is active.

At a certain moment you will feel, you will realize, that you are not only generating centrifugal forces, but centripetal ones also, like in a centrifuge. At the moment when you are in a condition of precarious equilibrium—that is, when your head is turned toward the zenith—the attraction, the pull, of the solar plexus will be so strong that your head will bend, will bow toward your solar plexus.

To incorporate this now into the practice: trace just one circle with your head, rather than continuous circles, highlighting the centrifugal forces as you exhale. You are exhaling, you are reaching out, as we have already seen. Then, when your head is turned toward the zenith, you start inhaling. That will draw your consciousness into the vacuum in the center of your body, the center of your life-field, that you access through the solar plexus. Your head bows toward the solar plexus as you begin the inhalation.

Think of the solar plexus as a threshold that gives you access into inverted space. This is where you are turning within. We have already discussed turning within, and reaching out from within. You then emerge out of that vacuum state reborn. There is a new dispensation released from the depths of your being. As you do that, your head moves upward. You transfer your attention from the solar plexus to your heart center.

The center of your being is no longer the solar plexus. It is the heart center. You do this while you continue to inhale. Your inhaling is divided into two halves. The first half begins when the head starts to come down. The second half begins when the head moves up slightly, contacting the heart center instead of the solar plexus. You hold your breath after inhaling.

Something very extraordinary happens at that moment. It is not samadhi, you are not departing from your existential condition. You are not lifting your head upward, no. The clue to it is that you are witnessing the alchemical marriage between spirit and matter. More specifically, just as in the Catholic Mass Christ is born, we are all born out of the encounter between the Holy Spirit and the virgin Mother Earth. Out of that encounter comes a new birth.

Think of the earth as being the immaculate state that you found in your solar plexus. For the descent, think of all that your being goes through in the course of your descent through the spheres, as it prepares to encounter all that the earth has to offer you after having developed it during the course of the eons of time. What a miracle birth is!

But this is a rebirthing, a recurrent rebirthing. You are celebrating the recurrent rebirthing. Let us say that those factors in your being that you could metaphorically ascribe to above your head, to your crown center, and those that you could metaphorically ascribe to your solar plexus, meet in your heart. That is where the new birthing takes place, when you hold your breath.

Of course, it is God who is reborn as you each time. Instead of thinking that you are being reborn, it is the whole universe that is continually birthing itself as you, and as each one of us.

There is a cleansing that takes place from within, toward within—a resorption in the void. There is also a cleansing that takes place at the periphery, as we have already seen. Those elements which are more internal get cleansed from within. The best way to do this is to imagine that you are a temple and the area around the sanctuary is being cleansed or purified.

There are walls, maybe zones, to the temple, which take care of insuring a certain amount of cleanliness within the temple. But purification is particularly important in the sanctum sanctorum, the holy of holies. That is where you need to allow anything that is not totally in keeping with your ideal of holiness to be re-sorbed in the void. It is only by rediscovering the immaculate condition of your being—like the voice of Caruso within its distortion—that you can be reborn again, or that God can be reborn as you. That is the meaning of the virginity of Mary, the mother of Christ. You will find in your solar plexus, if you attune yourself to that internal state, that it is like a child. It is very vulnerable, trusting, and defenseless. That is why you had to have all the defenses at the periphery. When you get closer in you are defenseless. The only way you can be purified is to let anything untoward be resorbed in the void.

We are discovering the child within, discovering it is still there within its distortion. You will get the impression that you are wearing a mask: that not only your body, but your personality, is like a mask protecting your real being. Your real being is defenseless and immaculate, and will, by dint of its encounter with the descent of the Holy Spirit—that is, all the influences of the heavenly spheres—be able to transform the more peripheral elements of your personality. That is why you think you are reborn: because you are transformed.

Another aspect of the solar plexus is that it is not only the child, but the blastema. The blastema is the original cell of the embryo before it is differentiated, so all of the qualities are present, the entire code of the DNA is there. At this stage there is no difference between those cells in which certain genes are active and other genes are recessive, and other cells. They are all the same. There is a fundamental unity. Diversity then develops as the cells proliferate. So you are touching upon a pristine condition. It is like starting all over again from scratch. A real rebirthing is a starting over from scratch; tabula rasa, a smoothed tablet, as you would say in Latin.

It is as though to be reborn all that you have acquired has to be relinquished. Otherwise your personality would be a collage; you would be trying to combine things that do not fit in nicely with each other. It has to be a fresh start. In a sense, it is almost easier to be nothing and to start again than to try to repair the damage. So that state, the state of the blastema, the Sufis call *imkan*, the state of all-possibility.

Then, of course, the possibilities are limited as diversity sets in. But remember that the state of all-possibility is present at the core of your being. That is, there is no limit to your potentialities. We limit them by not believing in them, by little faith. And, of course,, by our blunders.

There is a still further aspect of the solar plexus, in fact there are another two. Again, we will need to change our way of thinking in order to explore these further aspects. When you are inhaling, you think that you are somehow ingesting the environment and transmuting it, sublimating it, distilling it. Yes. But there is another aspect of it which Pir-o-Murshid shows us. The elements of what he calls the abstract are drawn into a center as you inhale. By "abstract" would be meant the elements of the latent potentialities rather than the elements of that which has actuated itself in the universe.

This is not the same thing as the convergence of the universe. That is something that we have considered when working with ourselves, that we converge the universe. It is a useful perspective. But now we want to consider the all-potentialities within the vacuum state in the center of our being. The word is *coagulate* rather than *converge*. Pir-o-Murshid illustrates it by the sun. Originally the light of the universe is diffused—he calls it the all-pervading light—and then, in order for existence to happen, this all-pervading light has to collect itself into a center, like the sun. Then it radiates from that center.[1]

As you are breathing in, instead of thinking that you are converging the universe, you could think that you are centering the bounty of your being into an active center which will eventually radiate. In the implicate state everything is everywhere, so in the void everything is interspersed with everything else. The transit takes place when, as David Bohm shows, the all-potentiality unfolds. A good example would be the way that the all-potentiality of radio waves gets processed by the radio into sounds, into discrete sounds.

So, the all-pervading light now draws itself into a point and then radiates as our aura. It is better to think in terms of radiating light than magnetism. When you transfer your attention to the heart center, on the second half of the inhalation, it is just like an explosion of radiance, of joy, of power.

Now you are waiting for what we call the descent of the Holy Spirit. It really requires you to recontact or reconnect with the heavenly spheres, because if you think in terms of being the recipient of the Holy Spirit, you are thinking in terms of duality. In the marriage there is no duality; there is a merging into the One. You have to be imbued with the sense of oneness. You have to

1 *The Inner Life*, vol. 1, *The Sufi Message of Hazrat Inayat Khan*, Centennial Edition, 164.

combine the two poles of your being. You need to be aware of the heavenly pole of your being, and not just think that you are the physical receptacle that is being quickened by the Holy Spirit.

So you are going to have to explore the heavenly levels of your being. We have been working with turning within and reaching out: the cosmic dimension. We are going to have to work much more with the transcendental level. We cannot do it all now, but we are anticipating the next step.

We are working with metaphors. You know that the only way in which a hologram can be projected is if you thrust a laser beam upon the light formations that are already there. That is something like the descent of the Holy Spirit. It is also the divine intelligence that brings it all into focus. The cosmic dimension is the hologram, and then the transcendental dimension is the laser beam that brings it all into focus. Think of that. As you hold your breath, think of a beam of light that triggers off the radiance of your aura.

You know that when your understanding clicks, your whole face lights up. In fact, your aura burns more brightly. That is the effect of the light of intelligence upon the radiance of the physical aura. When you hold your breath, that is the moment of awakening in life instead of beyond life. It is not samadhi, it is awakening in life.

In this marriage we see the mind-body connection, which does not mean that the mind depends upon the body to know. We would like to highlight these words of David Bohm: be not surprised if a sudden click in your understanding is going to fray new circuits in your brain.[2] If we are carrying impressions of the world that are faulty right in the cells of our brain—and that is what we are doing all the time—the circuits in our brain are in a bad condition. They are in a state of dismay. It is not surprising that we goof, because everything is based upon those impressions that are all wrong to start with. We did not check them before they formed pathways within the cells of our brain.

Any new realization is going to alter the pathways and bring them into a more meaningful circuitry, a new configuration. That is the way the laser beam acts upon the hologram. It brings congruence into what at first is an incongruent or random situation. This is what you experience as you hold your breath.

Everyone in the world is according to his or her realization. The body, and even the mind, are the underpinnings.

Those are the thoughts that lead toward illumination. Of course, do not be surprised if a change in your body condition triggers off new realizations in your understanding. That is why you invite the body to participate in your realization in the act of the zikr. There are many factors here which we need to go into. By drawing your attention to a particular plexus of the nervous system—that is what the chakras are—you are affecting your body. The Tibetans say that the body is a marvelous instrument in which to promote awakening, providing you transform it. You are transforming your body by your practices.

---

2 David Bohm, *Unfolding Meaning*. This work comprises an overview of Bohm's whole philosophy. His distinguished career combines research into physics and philosophy, and he worked closely with both Einstein and Krishnamurti.

For example, by concentrating on the solar plexus you are affecting your pancreas. You are setting a lot of endocrine glands into action, because they are all connected. By concentrating on the crown center you inject beta endorphin into the blood system. You are affecting the body, and that in turn will affect your realization. It works both ways. As a matter of fact, by reaching very deep into the solar plexus you are affecting the adrenal glands, which send shock waves throughout the whole system and trigger off a rebirthing.

There is a further realization that you need to have, or that is helpful, in order to make the best use of this wonderful practice. Think of your mind or psyche as being at the periphery of your being. You reach a level of your being deeper than the mind level or the psychological level, deeper than the level of the psyche. That does not mean the unconscious, because the unconscious is all part of the psyche. You can say that the conscious is just that part of the psyche that is illuminated by your awareness. But we are speaking of a deeper level of your being.

If you are a physicist or scientifically minded, you will recognize what is now called the scalar level, a deeper level of reality which is typified by its precariousness. It takes very little energy to shift the system. You have a level of reality that is so sensitive that it can shift easily from one condition to the other. This is the precarious equilibrium that Prigogine is speaking about. This is where creativity starts.

As you turn within, you discover how vulnerable the core of your being is, how easily it can shift one way or the other. The advantage of it is that it is open to all-possibility. There is no limitation because there is no resistance. You see that your creativity consists of fluctuations from that precarious equilibrium. Therefore, you need to be very, very fine-tuned. The word used is *latif*, which means "fine," and also the Latin word *implicare*, which means "finely-woven." Everything is in contact with everything else. It is a very fine setting, a pristine state.

Instead of thinking of repairing the faulty condition of your psyche, it is better to think in terms of a new birthing from that precarious state. It is very important for psychotherapists to see that. That is the difference between *mu'id* and *muhyi. Mu'id* would be repair, therapy. *Muhyi* is regenerating, we could even say turning the table on the handicap. We are using the word *handicap*; it is a much better word than *disability*, because a handicap is an obstacle that you can overcome, whereas disability sounds absolutely final.

Turn the tables on your infirmities. Use them as ladders to become better than you were prior to the infirmity. A rebirthing always starts with the perfect many-splendored totality of genes. There is no limitation in the beginning, at the inception of creativity. It is only as it is carried further that limitation sets in.

The secret of this is to really believe in what the Sufis call our divine inheritance. Perhaps the word *believe* is not the right word. There is a difference between faith and belief. Frequently, you believe because somebody said it. But faith is like trusting your intuition, even when it is continually being questioned by your reasoning.

There comes a time when you do not need to make the motion of the zikr anymore, or coordinate your breath with the motion. If the different attunements are clear in your realization, you are encouraging their operation by your awareness.

You become very sensitive while you are meditating, and, if you are in that precarious condition, you see how your thoughts affect the attunement of your soul right away. You see how the attunement of your soul affects your relationship with the environment. So you do not choose just any meditation theme.

You started by considering your problems instead of an artificial object. But now it is your attunement and your realization that are the objects of your meditation. You are at a very high level of awareness. You are not struggling with random thoughts anymore. It does not matter; the thoughts just do what they have to do. They are on the periphery, but that is not where you are concentrating.

Chapter 6

Surveying the Planes

There is another dimension of awakening which we are going to explore: that is awakening in the transcendental dimension, in contrast to the cosmic dimension. You could think of these as latitude and longitude, two dimensions that are interdependent.

When you are meditating it is important to remember, to keep reminding yourself, "I am training myself with an objective in view, and that objective is to awaken." Pir-o¬Murshid said every atom, every planet, every being in the universe is awaiting the moment of awakening.[1] Think of it as a sudden breakthrough, like, for example, the chick breaking out of the egg. That is the meaning of satori, a sudden jerk as it were. Awakening could be defined as a sudden change of perspective. You cannot transit between the two, the unawakened state and the awakened state: there are no transitional stages. It is either one or the other. Let us ascertain this for ourselves.

Imagine that you have drawn a cube on a blackboard, and you see it from a certain perspective. Then you change your perspective. Do you see what I mean? You can look at it one way, or the other. That would be

1 Inayat Khan, *Mastery through Accomplishment*, 302.

an example of being able to change a perspective, and alternate between two perspectives, toggle between the two. You could practice this by seeing the cube from one perspective as you exhale, and the other perspective as you inhale.

Let us give an example of a change of perspective which would be a good indication of the difference between the cosmic dimension and the transcendental. We have already said that these dimensions are related, that they are interdependent. The difference between them would be indicated by walking in a landscape which is extremely vast, as compared with being enclosed in your room. That will give you a sense of the extension of your perspective. The cosmic dimension includes two aspects: expanse and turning within. To understand what we mean by turning within, imagine walking in a forest. It does not have to be a forest, it could be the mountains. It could be anywhere that you find yourself in a transfigured world, or seeing that which transpires behind that which appears. For example, the way the photographs of Walter Chappell show aspects of the flowers that you cannot see in ordinary light. They are photographed in ultraviolet light.[2] That would be an indication of what we mean by the cosmic perspective.

But now suppose that you are flying in the space shuttle, and you are so high that you have a real overview of the whole planet. You can see the planet in its

---

2 Walter Chappell (1925–2000) placed plants on the surface of a photographic plate in complete darkness, without lens or camera. "When this living organic matter is introduced into a high voltage field, its electrons are changed into photons, and for a sparkling instant They produce an image of the plant's life force." See appendix.

relationship with the starry sky, instead of your usual viewpoint from the planet. That would certainly be a change of perspective. That would illustrate to some extent what we mean by the transcendental dimension. Call it overview.

The cosmic dimension would be the ability to see the relationship between two things whose relationship you just had not seen before. Typical of that is the intelligence test for a monkey. There is a banana outside the cage, and a stick in the cage. At a certain moment the monkey sees the relationship between the two. That is a very primitive form of awakening: seeing the relationship between two things that you had not seen before. That is what we have been focusing on in the preceding chapters.

The advantage of the implicate state, the jumbled state where everything is interspersed with everything else, is that things are in such close contact that you can more easily see a relationship between them. One of the aspects of the cosmic dimension, which is typical of turning within, is the dream state. The mind in its everyday, normal mode does not know how to deal with these impressions that are not discrete impressions; they are all jumbled. But the consequence is that you can see a meaningfulness there that you cannot see when things are too segregated.

Awakening in the transcendental dimension would be illustrated by a concept that is rather unfamiliar in the West, but which you find in Vedanta: awakening in deep sleep. That is the way that samadhi can best be described. It is a state in which you acquire a sense of the programming behind the universe. Another example would be the difference between visiting a building accompanied by the architect, who explains how it all works; or just visiting the architect's office and seeing the blueprints. The transcendental dimension of awakening would be simply knowing the blueprints, and not necessarily how it all works.

That is the key, those two forms of knowledge. There are two awakenings according to Pir-o-Murshid Inayat Khan: awakening beyond life, and, then, awakening in life. What Pir-o-Murshid calls wisdom is born out of the combination of these two awakenings.[3]

A further example would be found in a painting by Leonardo da Vinci. Behind that painting there is a lot of patterning, a lot of thinking. It is as though there were deep patterns behind the gloss at the surface, patterns based upon the golden mean and certain mathematical principles. Or, if you study a prelude by Chopin, you find that there is a lot of thinking behind it; there are certain geometrical patterns, mathematical progressions, numerical progressions. Having insight into that kind of configuration—let us say the way that pure understanding can configure itself in form—would give you some clue as to awakening in life.

But awakening in the transcendental dimension would be grasping the intention. Why does Leonardo da Vinci base his painting upon this pattern? What is his intention? Pir-o-Murshid describes awakening as grasping the intention behind the universe.[4] This is the reason why the Sufis say you are invited to the court of the king—that is, you are allowed to understand something of

3 *In an Eastern Rose Garden*, vol. 7, *The Sufi Message of Hazrat Inayat Khan*, 234–35.
4 *Sufi Teachings*, vol. 8, *The Sufi Message of Hazrat Inayat Khan*, 303.

the strategy. There is both awakening in life and awakening beyond life, and they are interdependent.

How does one trigger off awakening in the transcendental dimension? There are meditation skills which will help you, as long as you are very clear that your objective is to have an overview rather than a comprehensive view. Be sure that you recognize the difference: an overview—that is, you can see what is intended behind it—rather than simply an overall view.

Let us start with very definite practices. For the cosmic dimension, if you remember, as you exhale you extend your consciousness into wider and wider fields. You think of stars. Or, you could do it in an even more gradual manner.

For example, imagine you are sitting in nature and your consciousness reaches out into the expanse of the immediate environment: the trees, the flowers, insects, some animals. Then your consciousness extends further, into a wider purview. Your consciousness extends beyond what you can see. Eventually, you think of the whole planet. Then your consciousness extends into the starry sky. And you think, "What I envision of the starry sky is only a very small section of the cosmos. The cosmos is far beyond what I could ever see, or what I could ever imagine." That is one way in which consciousness can be extended in space.

You could also extend it in time. You could think, "This body already existed in the stardust at the beginning of time, and has been molded in the course of eons of time." You could think of the whole history of the universe; that, again, has the effect of extending your consciousness. Whereas, in the past, and even perhaps now to some extent in some places, people who are just confined to a village have no idea about the whole, the immensity of the procession of time.

This extension of consciousness should be combined with an extension of your notion of yourself. If you think of yourself as a magnetic field, that will already give you a wider sense of yourself than is usually the case. And if you think of yourself as an aura, it will give you a still wider sense of yourself; you find yourself interspersed with the light of the stars.

We added to this, if you remember, Pir-o-Murshid's contribution to this practice: you become clear about the outreach of your being, how it affects people and situations around you. He calls it your domain.[5] You will begin to have a sense of the impact of your being upon the universe as a whole, your contribution toward, let us say, the great drama that is enacted in the universe. That would be the cosmic dimension.

To work with the other aspect of the cosmic dimension, if you remember, we turn within and hold our breath. We reach out from inside, we start thinking from the point of view of other people, and soon. That is a complementary perspective to the wider one.

In order to foster awakening in the transcendental dimension, you transfer your attention from the bottom of the spine upward as you inhale. With the cosmic dimension, when you held your breath you concentrated on the solar plexus. Now you move all the way up your spine as you inhale, and concentrate above the head as you hold your breath. Shift your attention down the spine as you exhale. That is, of course, an elementary practice.

5 *Healing and the Mind World*, 221.

At a further step, you continue moving up, concentrating your attention spatially upward, after you have reached the top of your head. As you hold your breath, it is just as we have said: Bellerophon rides Pegasus on the way toward Olympus, and, at a certain moment, Pegasus cannot fly any higher and Bellerophon has to continue on his own.

So, imagine that your breath is Pegasus, and it is carrying your consciousness upward. At a certain moment, your breath cannot carry you any further, but it has imprinted upon you a momentum. You take advantage of that momentum to rise into the higher spheres. Turn your eyeballs upward as you hold your breath.

We will need to follow this up by exploring and being aware of the different planes, otherwise we could get ourselves lost in a very vague state, a kind of unknowing.

As you exhale, then, try to reminisce, try to recollect, your descent through the spheres. One way of doing this would be to think that you are a denizen from outer space. You have landed on the planet in order to experience conditions on the planet, and even to have some impact on the planet. Consequently, you experience, or, you explore, your interconnection with the health of your body, and with bodiness in general—which is the fabric, not just of the planet, but of the whole universe.

It is not just a question of transferring your attention from one chakra to the next as you rise. You shift your sense of identity. This is one of the clues. You feel like an etheric body, and then you feel like a being of light. Those are elementary steps.

A more advanced way of doing this, of shifting your sense of identity, is to be more precise, to be as clear as possible. You realize that your thinking can be related to matter. Think of things which involve matter: if you are a carpenter, you work with wood; or even, if you are a musician, your dealings would be with sound as matter. But you can also reach a point when matter does not enter into configuration. There are different levels of thought.

That gives you a clue as to how to awaken in the transcendental dimension: if, while you are meditating, you shift your thinking so that it is not connected with any representation of the physical world—for example, if you are contemplating a divine name. That is one of the steps: to not be thinking about either a material object or even a spatial configuration. The consequence is that your thinking shifts upward into the transcendental dimension, and it has an immediate effect upon your sense of identity.

We start off by thinking in terms of space, as in the formulation We are lifting our consciousness upward. At a certain moment space is not relevant anymore; and, if you still think in terms of hoisting yourself up in space, you will get into an astral state, which is not meditation. The clue is to realize that the notion of space is associated with matter.

In order to awaken in the transcendental dimension you have to shift your thinking so that space is not relevant anymore, nor time. The consequence is that you discover having always existed, and you are not located in space. At a certain level, space has no relevance.

The clue is to be found in the words of Pir-o-Murshid: you can raise yourself at will from your earthly condition.[6] The way to do it is to consider that your sense of

6 *The Alchemy of Happiness*, 74.

identity is just a condition. That is the right word: it is a condition, just like the wave of the sea is a condition of the sea. So, you shift your sense of identity from being an earthbound being. That is how reminiscences of your heavenly condition begin to surface in your memory.

That is the meaning of being the son or daughter of God, instead of being the son or daughter of your parents. As long as you think of yourself as the person who is living in that house and doing this job, or the son or daughter of these parents and ancestors, and so on, you will never be able to awaken. That is where most people are at.

It might be helpful to think of yourself as being like some birds—storm petrels, for example—who live most of the time in the sky. They descend to the earth just to catch a fish, and then continue soaring in the sky.

Now, of course, we have to alternate between inhaling and exhaling; and you even hold your breath between those two. When you exhale, you become aware of the miracle of your involvement with the fabric of the planet, or the fabric of the universe, in your own body.

This connection is so paradoxical that there is no way of explaining it. But it comes very strongly to view when you ask yourself, "How is it that if I think of moving my arm, it moves? How can I move this flesh by an act of my mind?" That connection is very deep; you would have to study physiology to see where and what that connection is: the firing of neurotransmitters, the hormones, and the whole inner structure—what we would call esoteric chemistry.

The fact is that matter is endowed with intelligence. You are communicating with the mind of the cells. Or you could say that the global mind of the body, of the person, is connecting with the mind of the cells and triggering off an action. That is more of an accepted view nowadays, the mind-body connection. But it is questioned whether the mind can function without the brain. We are saying that, where matter is involved, our mind has to follow certain patterns; there are certain constraints. But the mind is able to deal with thoughts in which matter is not involved.

That is a philosophical question, a metaphysical question. In practice, we would say that in order to awaken, think that you can think without a brain. You were thinking before you were conceived or endowed with a body, and you continue to think after the dissolution of the body. The body provides you with a very good support system, but, just like Pegasus, you can do without it. At a certain point you can do without it.

It is when you are holding your breath that your consciousness soars. But do not think that it is soaring upward in space. To avoid doing that, we need to have some kind of indication of the different spheres, or planes, within which we exist. When your attention has shifted above your head and you hold your breath, you continue soaring—but not in space. You are shifting from one sphere to another rather than soaring in space.

In order to gain a sense of the first sphere, the plane named *nasut*, think of yourself as being made of subtle matter. Thinking of yourself as a being of light—not physical light, but as a being of light—will free you in your mind from the sense of physical matter located in

93

space and time. You were a being of light prior to your birth or to your conception, and you will continue to be so. We are not talking about physical light.

Since space has no relevance here, obviously the light of your being does not have a boundary and is not located anywhere in space. We are so used to thinking in terms of being located in space and time, and being made of fabric, of matter—it is very difficult to overcome that habit of thinking, and to shift our sense of identity. That is a clue of course: to free yourself from your habits of thinking. There are methods, and we will indicate a method to you.

Imagine that you have set off on a journey into outer space. Nowadays it has been done, and it is perfectly feasible. You make a space walk, which is also feasible. But beware of thinking, "How wonderful to see these stars and see the planet right out there in space." If you think of yourself as an aura, and you think that the stars converge as your aura, then the stars are no longer the object of your cognizance. You are the light of the stars. Your whole sense of identity has shifted—from being the observer, from being the individual, and also from being located in space and, of course, situated in time.

These are exercises of the imagination, the power of imagination, that exert a very strong stress upon our commonplace assumptions. You have to really jolt yourself out of your commonplace assumptions in order to awaken. Awakening is always a sudden shift of perspective.

We can be thankful that we are living at that time when Joseph Campbell has made us aware of the value of myth.[7] The second plane is called *mithal*. It lifts us

---

7 Joseph Campbell (1904–87) taught at Sarah Lawrence College and published numerous works. He is largely responsible for

above the perfunctory level of the commonplace experience. We discover a level of our thinking which we neglect in our flattened-out universe. The ancients used to feel more comfortable with myth than the way we have been conditioned to be in our materialistic society.

It is important to realize that our minds think like the universe thinks. If it were otherwise, we could never understand the universe. Consequently, at some level of our thinking the universe thinks as our thinking, in the mode of our thinking. This takes place at the level of metaphor. That would compare with the kind of thinking that goes on in a composer's mind before his or her thinking materializes into notes, and rhythms, and orchestration. The B Minor Mass of Bach is a myth, and it materializes in notes. Originally, it is a myth.

For the time being we are going through these planes, just a kind of sampling. We will have to do it a little more in depth later on. The next plane, *malakut*, is really like an awakening—all of a sudden you remember, you think of yourself as a fallen angel. That is a very good term. One of the ways of doing this is to discover the child within you. You see that the child is still there within the mature person. Of course, the mature person has developed qualities that were latent in the child, that had not yet come to the surface. But it is that defenseless, vulnerable, idealistic aspect of your being which will give you access into the heavenly spheres.

For example, in meditation or while on retreat you may feel you have participated in the cosmic celebration in the heavens. You come back to your earthly condition,

bringing an awareness of myth into contemporary culture. One of his works bears the title *The Inner Reaches of Outer Space: Metaphor as Myth and as Religion* (New York: Van der Marck, 1986).

to your job and the people around you, the supermarket, and so on; and you think, "Good God, what a fall. I have forgotten who I am." It is incredible—not just what a fall, but what ignorance. Although, if we were not ignorant, maybe we would not go about doing the material things we do, and we would starve.

So perhaps that is the way we are programmed, to be ignorant. But awakening is, of course, contrary to ignorance, a reversal of that ignorance. It is difficult to be an awakened person and to deal with the nitty-gritty of life. Yet, that is what we are called upon to do. We are protected by our ignorance until such time that we do not need that protection any more.

All these levels, these spheres, are transitional: each is a transition between the level above it and the level below it. At the level called *malakut*, the celestial plane, there is still some kind of configuration. It is not exactly a form, there is no profile. The word *countenance* comes to mind, the expression of the face rather than the face—like the photos of Walter Chappell. But to reach higher than the plane of the angels you have to give up any sense, any residue, of what we understand by form.

The keyword for that next sphere is *splendor*, the realm of splendor. Buddha speaks about the beings of pure splendor: no form, no consciousness—intelligence, but not consciousness. We call the plane of pure splendor *jabarut*.

It is obvious that this level is only accessible through emotion, the attunement of our emotions, rather than through our will or our understanding. Let yourself be carried by an image, an impending sense of bliss, which we are usually soft-pedaling in our lives. We are not expecting splendor. We choose pebbles rather than pearls. There is no accounting for taste.

It is sublime emotion—not the emotion of your personal anger or resentment or satisfaction, but sublime, impersonal emotion—that will hoist your consciousness from the celestial plane into the level of jabarut. At that level, your sense of being an individual, a discrete individual, gets dissolved. In fact, you have lost any sense of identity. You do not know who you are. You have a sense of having allowed yourself to be fooled by your sense of identity, by the appearance of things, by your involvement in the material world. In fact, life on earth seems to be a dream.

There are higher spheres, but you might feel dizzy to have reached this altitude. Anything that we could say about further levels would be just words; it would be theory instead of reality. You find utterances of mystics that convey something of the further levels.[8] Ultimately, of course, is the divine intention. You can have a computer program, but the program is customized according to what your goals are. The intention is a higher level than the programming. So, discovering the programming of the universe is already quite exciting; but the intention behind that, the divine intention— that is shattering to our understanding.

If we attempt to translate such experience into something our understanding can grasp, it seems very trite. As, for example, The whole purpose of life is love, the divine love. Well, that is the best way that we can say it. But if we actually love, rather than talk about love,

---

8 See for example, 'Abd al-Qadir Jilani, *Utterances*, and Fakhr ad-Din Iraqi, *Divine Flashes*.

then it will make the ultimate and utmost sense. It will convey the utmost meaning.

Perhaps we could use the word "generosity," which is almost better than love. An example of generosity would be if parents were not only to wish that their son or daughter should be a wonderful replicate of themselves, but if they should wish that a son or daughter should be better than themselves. That is the meaning of *rahmaniat*: it is the intention behind the whole thing. A very good model of this would be to imagine that God—this is just a model of course; it might help us to understand something beyond our own minds—that God hopes that the children will excel God's own Self, also.

There is a saying of Saint Augustine, that God becomes human so that humanity becomes God.[9] That is the intention behind it all. Think of God as dynamic rather than static; God in the process of becoming as us, rather than having existed in a perfect state, of which we are simply a very poor replicate. That is the meaning of *Dhu'l Jalal wa'l-Ikram*: God in the process of becoming God, as us; not through us, but as us.

The clue to this level, which is called *lahut*, is to be found in the words of Pir-o-Murshid Inayat Khan:, that God discovers God's own perfection in our imperfection.[10] You can discover the voice of Caruso in its distortion. When we awaken, we discover the divine perfection through our imperfection. We are able to hoist ourselves above our earthly condition. We have to identify ourselves with our perfection, which is the

9 Augustine (354–420), a Christian theologian and a Neoplatonist, reconciled Christianity and Greek philosophical thoughts.
10 Inayat Khan, *Song of the Prophets*, 109–10.

divine perfection within our imperfection, instead of dwelling upon our imperfection, which keeps us in our earthly condition.

You can see that if we are using the words *perfection* and *imperfection,* we are still talking in terms of multiplicity. Lahut is the level of archetypes. But there is a level beyond, which is called *hahut,* where all sense of multiplicity has disappeared. You cannot say you see the unity because you merge into this unity. This is articulated in the words of al-Hallaj: *ana'l-Haqq!* (I am Truth!) That refers to the one and only I. You discover yourself as the divine spectator, instead of the means whereby the divine qualities are actuated.

Perhaps we could end this review of the planes with our rendering of the Hadith which is at the center of all Sufism.[11] In the tradition, Sufi teachers do make their own commentaries. Ibn 'Arabi made his, for example. Ours is God speaking: "I was an unknown treasure and I loved to be known"; so it is not "I desired to be known, or to know myself." And in order to do this I became, in the consciousness of all beings, the subject of my self-discovery; and, in the nature of all beings, the object of my self-discovery. That is where duality comes into the picture: in order to fulfill the divine intention. But, originally, there exists just a hidden treasure. Both subject and object are enacted within the ultimate unity.

That is the reason why, in Vedanta, the objective is unity beyond duality. Vedanta and Sufism are the same.

---

11 The hadith upon which Pir Vilayat is commenting is generally stated "I was a hidden treasure, and I longed to be known," and may be understood as an answer by God to the question: What was the purpose of creation?

Chapter 7

Stages of Samadhi

We need to do practices in order to apply the things which we have been considering. First, be very clear about this: to awaken, you have to be extremely alert. Some people seem to be half dead, in a vague kind of trance state, when they are meditating. You want to be very aware and very alert. There is nothing of a trancelike state in an awakened being. To be very aware means seeing behind the curtain, seeing what is being enacted in the drama of life.

What are we looking for in awakening? We would like to see ourselves in the universe, to see our purpose. We realize that there is no way of encompassing this with our ordinary thinking. We have a sense that somehow we are deceived, we are allowing ourselves to be deceived, by the appearance of things. So, really, awakening is to unmask the hoax of maya. There is no doubt about that. It requires a jolt, the unleashing of energy, a breakthrough of energy. Pegasus represents the energy of our being that carries consciousness beyond its middle-range—just like Einstein imagining what it would be like to ride on a photon at the speed of light.

There is a phrase used by the Tibetans: the mind rides the wind. Always think of that: there is always energy underpinning, supporting, our consciousness. For our consciousness to rise into higher levels, we have to use finer energy. The Tibetans say that also; they speak about different levels of energy, and the different modes of thinking which correspond to each level of energy. When we worked with transferring our consciousness from one chakra to the next, we were awakening the energy corresponding to each level, the energy of each chakra.

Each chakra represents a certain level of energy. You can, for an example, think in terms of a gong: by striking it, you awaken it. The word "awakening" applies here to unleashing energy. The gong is already resonating in a way that we cannot hear. The molecules and the atoms are already jiggling, but, by hitting it, you are impacting it with a new force. The consequence is that, due to the mutual resonance between the different atoms, these atoms begin to cohere with one another and form definite frequency-wave patterns. So you are striking the gong to awaken it.

In the same way, think that you need to strike the whole composition of energies in your being in order for your consciousness to awaken.

Another example would be to imagine a flame arising in your spinal cord. Think of your spinal cord as a chimney, and there is a flame that rises within it. At the bottom of the flame it is red, and as it moves upward you get orange; and then yellow, and then green, and then blue—all of the colors of the spectrum. Just thinking of those colors will help you shift energy levels as you inhale. You are awakening faculties within yourself simply by the power of mind over matter, by the power of imagination.

The other way of looking at it is imagining that in sleep you wake up from day consciousness, instead of thinking that you wake up from sleep into day consciousness. The technique used consists in maintaining yourself at the threshold between day consciousness and sleep—sleep with dreams—so that reminiscences of the world seem to linger in your memory, but it is rather like an echo.

You remember a very small fraction of the extraordinary richness which you are perceiving all the time. If you try to remember, for example, the way that it looked walking in the snow, you realize that what you remember is very little in comparison with the richness of the environment. Still, that memory lingers in your psyche. It is very important to know that the world continues to live in our psyche. Our psyche is furnished with the impressions of the world. They are embedded in our psyche; they continue to live there and function, and then cross-pollinate with other impressions.

What is more, the representation that we make of the physical world is, if not false, at least very poor. It is very inadequate. Your psyche is furnished with a lot of stuff that does not ring true. This continues to persist in your dreams. You dream of impressions that were not well dealt with in your day consciousness. As we have already seen, the dream state is the implicate state of the mind. All those impressions are jumbled with one another, and so you move, by the process of association, from one to another without much coherence.

Do you see how, in the dream state, you have lost the handle on your cohering mind? In other words, you have lost the sense of congruity. The mind is trying to see connections that are beyond its usual ability. That is why the impressions in dreams are so confused. If you maintain yourself at the threshold, you are aware, but vaguely aware, of the impressions of the physical world. One of the things that you can do when you are meditating is to let the input of impressions from the physical world become more and more remote. It seems like it is there somewhere, but you cannot quite reach it. You remember it, but you are not experiencing it. That is the first stage in the samadhi practices.

The way to cast the impressions a little further from your consciousness is to think that they are misleading. In some way, you are devalidating your assessment of the physical world, and the same thing is true of your problems. You do remember your problems; or rather, what you remember is your assessment of your problems. It is not your problems, it is your assessment.

Convince yourself that your assessment cannot be absolute, so it must be relative; and probably it is totally off. The consequence is that the grip these problems bear upon your consciousness is weakened. Now the problems seem a little bit nebulous, and, in fact, the whole physical world seems a little bit nebulous. That is what happens when you are about to go to sleep, when you are at the threshold.

If you shift from this threshold a little bit toward the dream state, then you will lose your memory of the physical world, except that it triggers off thoughts, creative thoughts, in your imagination. The memories of events in the physical world act as catalysts that arouse images and thoughts that do not seem to tally completely. Your emotional frustrations are triggered off by residue of the memory of everyday life, perhaps through the process of association. In the dream state, unevolved desires, or disappointments, or frustrations try to make themselves known to you by configuring themselves into forms, or even scenarios. It is not always clear what these configurations mean.

For example, all of a sudden you see your passport, and you do not understand the dream. The dream may be telling you that you want to be a little more clear about your identity. Or you see a horse: that may represent an outbreak of energy that has been withheld.

The residue of the impressions from the outer world is going to trigger off creative imaginings. The imaginings themselves, the forms that they take, are only devices through which deeper levels of your being are trying to make themselves known to you. If you are at the threshold you are able to see that connection. That is already a level of awareness that we cannot reach if we are simply caught up in the physical scene of the world.

There are impressions that are trying to come through from the depths of our being. But if we are emotionally attached to our problems, or our frustrations, or our desires, then such images will dominate over the impressions that are trying to come through from the heavenly spheres. It is clear, it is obvious now, that if you want to hoist your consciousness into what is called samadhi, into awakening, you need to first do a lot of clearing in connection with your personal desires. That is probably the reason why Buddha says that the way toward nirvana is to be desireless, to be without desires.

This seems to go counter to all that we said about wishing to build a beautiful world of beautiful people. Somehow, it frequently seems, in the measure to which you are involved in building this beautiful world, you

wish to pursue personal gain or a personal advantage—
or at least what you think is a personal advantage. But,
if you are able to avoid slipping into that purely ego-
tistical quest, then you can pursue fulfillment in life
with the objective of attaining excellence. You can still
seek accomplishment in life while being a dedicated
person—in which case you will not be bogged down
by your emotional frustrations.

So the key to having access to the heavenly levels of
your being is to pursue action, without your action
being dictated by concupiscence. The consequence is
that the whole area of frustrated desires is going to clear
itself. But the key to it is *vairagya*, that word you find
in India, which means detachment and indifference.
Pir-o-Murshid says: "Indifference and independence
are the two wings that enable the soul to fly.[1]" Also,
indifference is a staircase that frees you from earthly ties
and gives you access into the heavenly spheres.[2]

We have been working with two things: on one hand,
fulfilling *'ishq Allah*, the nostalgia to build a beautiful
world of beautiful people; and on the other hand, detachment. Now we are coming to realize that the ego
enters the picture when you are trying to accomplish
things, unless you become very clear as to what your
motivations are. That is why the beginning of any
meditation, according to Sufis, is called *muhasaba*:
confronting your conscience, rather than working with
consciousness; asking yourself: "What are my motivations? Why am I doing this?"

If you do not make this examination of conscience,
then there is a lack of clarity in your dreams. You are

1 Inayat Khan, *The Complete Sayings*, 19.
2 *The Inner Life*, 117–19.

ambiguous; there is a kind of ambiguity in your objectives in life. As soon as you have had the courage to face your intentions—that is where you apply the name *ya haqq*, Truth—everything seems to fall into place in your psyche. The Sufis call it the clarification of the mirror. That is when you begin to awaken in sleep instead of being held back by all the stuff that you still have to digest. That is why in Vedanta there is a distinction made between deep sleep and sleep with dreams.

In Vedanta, samadhi is typified by awakening in deep sleep. There are no images. You are bypassing what is called creative imagination, the faculty of the mind to project images. And when you do that while remembering the events of everyday life, you unmask the hoax. You are no longer simply recollecting them the way they appeared.

This is illustrated by the example of walking in the forest at night. You think you see a snake. The next day you walk the same path, and you see that it is a rope. Then the next night you walk the same path again, and you see that, indeed, it really does look like a snake—but you know now that it is not a snake. So, you are remembering the events of the day, but unmasking the hoax while remembering them. Therefore, the memory of them does not invade and pollute your psyche.

That is the first stage in the *Yoga Sutra* of Patanjali. Let us put it this way: when you start meditating, if you try to control your mind you are fighting a losing battle, because the mind is stronger. You cannot control it. And, it is counterproductive to stifle the dynamism of the mind. If you start meditating, and you do not try to control the mind but rather to give vent to the cosmic dimension of your emotion, then you think to yourself: "What a marvel this world is!"

Actually, all of this is tied up with our concept of God. We have got to be very clear about this. Somehow or other, awakening means getting into the thinking of the universe; it involves accessing the thinking of the universe. You must have a clear sense of what you mean by God. These are concepts, but you remember what Pir-o-Murshid said: our concept of God is the stepping stone to our experience of God. Be very careful not to confuse God with your concept of God. But still, you need to start with a concept and then realize that it is totally inadequate.

The concept of God that seems the most acceptable in our time would be that the whole universe is a being; that the physical cosmos is the body of that being, and our body is part of that body; that the universe thinks, and our thinking is part of the thinking of that being, the thinking of God; and the universe emotes, that is, has emotions, and we participate in these emotions; that the universe has consciousness, and we participate in this consciousness; and that you cannot limit this being to a physical body or even just a mind. You would have to include the angelic levels, for example.

Furthermore, that being is not only conscious but intelligent. Intelligence represents the ground of consciousness, so it is a deeper reality than consciousness. There is always duality in consciousness—subject, object—whereas intelligence is beyond that duality. Ultimately, whatever concept that we make of. God is totally inadequate. We must beware of limiting God to our concept of God. That is the reason why, in most religions, there is an emphasis on transcendence: that means beyond any concept that we can make of God. Yet, we need to make that concept.

In some way, our awakening is related to the condition of God. You might think, if you want, the condition of the universe; that is a limited way of thinking of God, but still, it is a step. You could look at awakening as accessing the thinking of the universe. And, if the universe is a conscious being, the universe delights in the discovery of its glory. So you participate in that ecstasy as you start meditating. In that case, you regard the physical world as being also God, instead of just thinking that God is beyond the physical universe. These are the ways of the mystics, not the way of a lot of religious dogmas.

That is looking at things from the point of view of the meditator. In Sufism, you are always looking at things from the antipodal standpoint of your personal standpoint. Or, rather, you are looking at things from both standpoints at the same time. From the divine standpoint, God is revealing God's own being, or nature, or—there is no way of saying this exactly in words—God's own Self, to each fragment of God's Self. The physical world, the way the physical world appears, is simply a bounty of clues or devices whereby the divine intention can be communicated—just as, for an example, the film *E.T.* was full of devices in which Spielberg communicated his intention as creator of the film. The reason why it makes sense to you is because the devices give you access into the thinking of Spielberg.

In the first stage of samadhi—called *sarvitarka samadhi*—you are trying to grasp reality. In the Sufi interpretation, all that you know is that which appears, or all that you know is the way things appear. That is, according to the Sufis, the *ayat*: the signs, the way that God manifests through signs. This is like the pugmarks of the bear in the snow; you have not seen the bear.

In one sense, if you take the pugmarks to be the bear then you are totally deceived. That is what we are doing all the time. If you consider it to be just clues, then it is not maya. It is maya if you take it to be real. If you take it to be ultimate, it is maya. If you see it as the means whereby God is revealing God's divine nature, then, of course, these are valuable clues.

Let us pursue this a little further. The layman's impression of the physical world is extremely poor in comparison to the insight that the physicist gets of the physical universe. In the next stage, *nirvetarka samadhi*, you are assimilating the picture of the physical world in your psyche. As we discovered earlier, you are furnishing your psyche with a false assessment of the physical world and of your problems. From the point of view of a psychotherapist this is very important. The psyche carries within it assessments of your problems that are faulty.

The first stage of samadhi is to grasp more deeply what the physical world really is. That is what physicists are doing. The kind of image of the physical world that physicists are carrying in their psyche is much more adequate than the image held by most people. For most people, what is much more relevant is the representation that they make, or the interpretation that they make, of their problems. This is the stage at which you need to question your assessment of your problems. You could even take it for granted that your assessment is wrong.

It is helpful not to be stuck in your assessment. Give your mind a chance to consider what it would be like if your assessment is wrong, if it is a misassessment. The consequence is that the stress of your representation of your problems upon your psyche will be alleviated. This burden which you are carrying, and which can be very, very heavy, gets lifted. Just imagine that you are carrying an unnecessary load that is totally built upon self-deception. Now that would be *nirvetarka samadhi*.

Let us put it this way, and make the whole circle: God reveals God's own being through devices. It could be physical objects; it could be situations. We are perceiving these, we are inputting these impressions; and we need to process that input. For example, if you do not break down the amino acid chains of your food by dint of your enzymes, then you are going to poison your body. Your body cannot take in those amino acids in the way that the food presents them. And just as the enzymes have an impact on the amino acid chain, there is a contribution of your idiosyncrasies to the way that you digest the impressions in your psyche.

If you just take in the amino acid chains without processing them, then you would have a terrible indigestion. That is what we are doing with our problems. You have to take into consideration the enzymes of your psyche, and those enzymes are your creative imagination. That is what you encounter when you are at the threshold between day consciousness and the dream state. There is a lot of work to do at this threshold, and, according to Yoga, you cannot lift yourself any further up the chain leading to *asamprajnata samadhi*—which is considered to be awakening—if you have not first dealt with this level.

As beings, one aspect of our job is to combine the disparate elements of the chaos in an orderly way. This is the work that we are doing with our mind; we are creating order in our mind. That means to never accept any kind of ambiguity in your mind. If you tend to dismiss things that you cannot understand, that will lead to a kind of lackadaisical attitude. That is why we say that meditation, at least in the first stages, basically consists of learning how to think.

In the first two stages of samadhi you can see the difference between the explicate state and the implicate state. The explicate would be *sarvitarka*, when you think of the world made up of discrete entities. Then, as it is integrated in the psyche, it is converted into an implicate state, where you see the relevance of things; this is *nirvetarka*. Remember what we discovered earlier: the sun and the moon are aligned, they are always aligned; but they only appear to be aligned from the vantage point of the earth at specific points in time.

There are two ways of going about this: either you imagine a vantage point other than the planet earth from which they would be aligned, or you imagine that their relationship does not have to be one of alignment. Typically, we only grasp those things that click. If our understanding extends, then we can grasp meaningfulness where things do not click. In the explicate state our minds can only see things when they click, but in the implicate state we see relationships that are not what they call rare events or singularities.

The next stage in awakening is called *sarvikara*, and following that is *nirvekara*. To describe *sarvikara samadhi* we use the Sanskrit word, *tanmatra*, which signifies the subtle reality. It is exactly what the Sufis mean by *ajsam*, the subtle body. This is much more real than we ordinarily imagine. The Tibetans call it the illusory body. It is not just that the physical scene is illusory, but our imagination is casting an illusion which is supposed to reveal what is behind it.

The whole universe is the creation of maya, which is imagination. At this level the Tibetans are shaping their subtle bodies, and that is something that we want to do as well: shaping our *ajsam* body, our subtle body, like a sculptor would do. If you think of your subtle body as being made of light, sculpting it is easier than if you are thinking of it as a magnetic field, or as what we mean by subtle matter.

Nirvekara samadhi would be that stage in which we find ourselves in a transfigured world. Instead of identifying with your physical body, identify yourself as a being of light. Walking in nature you will all of a sudden find that the whole of nature seems transfigured. You are living in a transfigured world. And you think to yourself: "Just imagine, I have been fooling myself all this time that the world was the way it looks. Now I realize that it is not at all the way that it looks."

Consider the photographs of Walter Chapell: they are much more real than the way the flowers look in everyday, ordinary light. When we see those photographs, we realize that we are fooling ourselves by thinking that flowers are the way that they look when they are photographed in ordinary light.

The way that God reveals the divine Self gets rather constrained in the physical forms of the world. It is much more malleable, and therefore conveys much more, in the form of our creative imagination. God reveals God's own Self to us through our creative imagination more readily than through the outer world—in music, or in whichever way we are creative.

In *nirvekara samadhi*, we are furnishing our psyche with our imaginings, rather than with the impressions of the outer world. Imagine Bach living with all his music! Your imaginings will aver themselves to be much more important than your impressions of the physical world, which you realize are inadequate. Those imaginings include the image that you make of yourself, your self-image, which keeps on being enriched if you allow the dream state to come through into your diurnal consciousness, your day consciousness.

That is what creativity is about. Music starts with a dream. Brahms had a dream. In his dream he heard a melody, and then it became a symphony, the Fourth Symphony. It started with a dream. Talk about dreams coming true: we can make our life a dream come true! That is how we adapt the world to our vision, instead of adapting ourself to the world.

The next stage is called *ananda samadhi*, and it corresponds to *malakut*, the celestial level. This can only be accessed through your ecstasy. Your ecstasy is the springhead behind your emotion. As there is no accounting for taste, so there are very gross emotions that will trigger off imaginings. That is why you have to be very sensitive about the nature of emotions if you want to access the heavenly spheres. There is a whole teaching of Buddha about this: he makes a very clear distinction between what he calls noble emotions and gross emotions; also between that pole of emotions which is personal and the one which is impersonal or universal. They are not different emotions; they are two poles of the same scale.

If you want to accede to the heavenly spheres, the personal emotions will not do it for you. If you get into the consciousness of Buddha meditating under the bodhi tree, then you will realize the power of cosmic emotion. It is like having your hand on the pulse of the universe. The devices are just devices; they are secondary in comparison with the springhead behind the devices, the emotional springhead.

You will find in yourself an impending sense of glorification. It is your mind, or your disappointments, or your wish for personal gain, which deter you from giving vent to that need for glorification. It is a very deep need, because, ultimately, we are created by our glorification. Our glorification is creative of our being. It is your sense of glorification that gives you access to the heavenly spheres; access, that is, that will unleash the memory of those spheres. Otherwise, you can try all you like and you will never be able to remember them by your will.

You allow yourself to be shattered in your emotions. The dervishes say that you are shattered and overwhelmed: *fana* and *baqa*, both at the same time. You cannot be the observer anymore. That is why Saint John of the Cross says the light is so blinding that it appears as darkness.[3] That is the dark night of the soul: there is a shattering, and then there is an overwhelming. The Tibetans call this a threshold.

---

3 John of the Cross, *The Dark Night of the Soul*, bk. 2, chap.8.

Throughout your meditations you still remember the physical world, but remotely. The physical environment and your self-image serve as a kind of anchor. But at this point there is a real blank out of your memory. Recall what the Tibetans say: while you are remembering, you unmask the hoax. You do not take it for granted that things are the way they appear.

At a certain moment even those reminiscences are wiped out altogether. You do go through a blank out. It seems like a death, actually. It is only possible if you are not afraid of death, otherwise you would turn back. This is where you may find the sudden eruption of the clear light of bliss.

That would be the celestial plane. There is a reminiscence of your celestial condition, and also of other beings.

Ibn 'Arabi says that in your high meditations you are invited into the company of angels—it is as though you were meeting. At that stage in your spiritual growth you have dreams of teachers, and prophets and saints; you dream of angelic beings and angelic scenes.

You could do it the other way around: before you go to sleep you could imagine these things, and this will open a door by what is called the process of association. This technique will be most beneficial if you have really cleared the ground floor.

Let me illustrate the technique with a story: a young lady told me that when she was a girl she had epilepsy. She had bad dreams, nightmares; and the doctor cured her by advising her to imagine beautiful landscapes before she went to sleep. Since she no longer had nightmares, she did not have any more fits of epilepsy.

We could pursue this a little further. Think of the words of David Bohm: be not surprised if a new sense of meaningfulness will fray new circuits in your brain.

We would also say that it conjures reminiscences of the deeper levels of our being—which is so important for your self-validation. If you do not have this knowledge of the depth of your being, then, limited to your earthly condition, your self-image is not only very poor but rather dismaying, even rather frightening. People go through terrible, terrible grief trying to cope with a self-image that is demeaning or denigrating. This level of self-knowledge, the remembrance of your celestial condition, is the safety buoy.

The ancients used to have these beautiful myths that kept this level of their being alive, even though it seemed like wishful thinking. But if you replace those images with dragons and dungeons, or whatever it is children are subjected to by TV, then you could understand that there is a lot of crime in the world. Those are the impressions with which their psyches are being furnished. That is what we are doing to our children—and then we are surprised that some of them turn out to be monsters.

There you see the importance of glorification—even just going to church, or praying the Muslim prayer, or going to the temple. It might seem, well, a bit childish; yes, we have grown up now, and it is all dogma and superstition. Yes. But it is a dramatization; it is the way in which we are trying to portray, in our very inadequate manner, the cosmic celebration in the heavens. This enables us to reconnect with the celestial level of our being, which is so important.

The level beyond *malakut* is called *jabarut*. It corresponds with what in Yoga is called the *asmita* level. *Asmita* is often referred to as your sense of identity, but you should not go too much by that interpretation. There is splendor in the thinking of the universe that triggers off emotion, celestial emotion; let us say splendor in the divine thinking. But these are words. At this level there is no way of defining it.

If you are able to eschew all sense of form—because imagination is the configuration of form, you are translating a thought or an emotion into a form—then you develop an insight into the whole universe. This is beyond imagination. You awaken in deep sleep, where there are no forms and no images. It is as though you are backstage of the universe and have access into the thinking behind it. It is not just the logic of this thinking that you realize; it is the splendor of this thinking. The scientists use the word "elegance": the elegance of the thinking behind the universe. There are clues to that in the laws of physics.

If you proceed further upward, then you find an absolute parallel between Yoga and Sufism. You discover *lahut*, which is the plane of the divine archetypes, like those that we invoke in our *waza'if* at the archetypal level. In Yoga, this is called *sabija*. *Bija* means seed; that is, you grasp the seeds behind what you think is reality. For example, a flower only manifests, or unfurls, a very small amount of the bounty that is present in the seed. If you go according to what you know of the physical world, you have no idea of the bounty that is lying in wait in the state of all-potentiality. *Imkan* means all-potentiality. This is the level of all-potentiality.

That is what Murshid means by the divine perfection. The extraordinary thing is when Murshid says discover your divine inheritance. This means to discover that you carry in your being the all-potential perfection that is waiting to be awakened. Murshid calls it awakening God within oneself. It is not just awakening in your understanding, but awakening God within one as oneself.

This is where the *waza'if* become very practical. Instead of thinking: "I want to develop a little more compassion," or "I want to develop a little more mastery," think: "I am the divine mastery and the divine compassion, but I am limiting it by not realizing that I am it, by refusing the divine gift of my divine inheritance out of false humility." We must stop thinking of God up there. You know the sort of thinking: Christ can be perfect but cannot be perfect. That is merely an excuse for not becoming the way we could be, if we would be what we might be.

Then we reach the plane of unity. There are clues. At this point, dervishes say things that seem to be fantasies. The dervish says, "All I see is God." We think there is something wrong with him, all he sees is God. That is a word of Baba Kule: "All I see is God." And even "I am God," which is the most preposterous thing you could ever say and the ultimate truth. But you must not say it, because you would be crucified by saying it. You only dare think it if you have lost your personal sense of being a separate entity.

Instead of trying to understand these words, let them percolate in you as you meditate. They will awaken certain things in you, perhaps in each person differently. Remember to be extremely alert. That does not mean conscious of the here and now, but conscious at all levels and, especially, conscious of the way that the everywhere-and-always manifests in the here-and-now.

Chapter 8

Working with Light

We need to bring all of these things a little more into focus. The best way to proceed is to start working with light, doing practices with light. We want to work like sculptors, sculpturing our aura so that we are able to make it the way we want it to be. This process is called embodying the states of consciousness.

The state of consciousness itself remains too unreal, too abstract. We wish for our realization to translate itself into a reality at the existential level, to become tangible. Our attunement or realization needs to assume a form. "All faces are God's face" is a saying from the Qur'an. Actually, it is the countenance that is coming through our face which reveals something of the divine nature.

This is a way of working more concretely with all that you have been trying to reach with your consciousness. Translate your attunement into tangible terms.

Start in a very elementary way: think that your body absorbs light from the environment as you inhale, and emits light into the environment as you exhale. That is perfectly feasible in terms of our knowledge of science. But what is particularly relevant here is the impact of mind over body.

That is, by consciously absorbing light, you absorb more light; and by consciously emitting light, you radiate more light. You are not reflecting light like a mirror. Rather, the very electrons in the atoms of your cells start dancing: they use the energy of light to free themselves from the constraint of their orbitals, and they start jumping from one orbital to another. It really is a kind of dance.

You can feel this: if you hold your breath between inhaling and exhaling, you will feel this wonderful surge of energy, the sparkling that occurs within the cells of your body. The electrons use up as much of the energy that has been absorbed as they can. Any remaining energy is then radiated as the aura.

Think of light as food. Food is energy, and energy gives one freedom. It is the freedom of the electrons that results in the radiance of the aura. In some sense, the radiance of your aura is related to your joy. If you are very sorry for yourself, you cannot radiate much light. Pir-o-Murshid said it this way: it is the unselfish person, that is, the person who is not that concerned about themselves, who can radiate more light.[1]

Now, instead of just thinking of radiating light, you can follow that light as it extends throughout the universe. A lovely thought to hold as you exhale is that your light is bombarding the stars. It is a fact that the photons of your aura are traveling through space at a speed of 186,000 miles a second. Can you imagine: 186,000 miles a second! Eventually they hit the stars.

There is another way of looking at it also: that the light of your aura is interspersed with the light of the

1 *Spriitual Liberty,* vol. 5, *The Sufi Message of Hazrat Inayat Khan,* 159.

stars, just as an eddy is interspersed with the wave-interference pattern at the surface of the lake.

In the second stage of this practice, instead of thinking of yourself as a body which absorbs light, identify yourself with your aura. You will find that, indeed, your aura is pulsing. It tends to contract as you converge the light of the stars with your inhalation. Your aura functions like a vortex, and the light of the stars, in a sense, gets drawn into the vortex. The light gets converged, centered, drawn in; and, as a consequence, there is a buildup of light. Then, as you exhale, that light spreads out.

The next practice to do is to work with the transcendental dimension instead of the cosmic. When you hold your breath after inhaling, you discover a fresh dispensation of light that emerges from within. You do not simply boomerang back the light that you have absorbed from the environment: you are adding to that a fresh dispensation of light. It is an entirely different dimension.

We would like to see how this fits into the current knowledge of physics. What Pir-o-Murshid is saying is this: light can be found in its explicate condition in the universe, as we imagine physical light; but in its implicate condition, where all the frequencies are jumbled, it is what Pir-o-Murshid calls the all-pervading light. What we mean by the all-pervading light is that it is not radiating from a center; it is jumbled, which is what we understand by the implicate state.

But what Murshid is saying is that you can, as you turn within, center that implicate, that all-pervading, light. You can draw it to the surface. What you do consciously is draw it from your solar plexus into your heart. It radiates from your heart. This light that is implicate, that is interspersed, or jumbled, is now drawn into a center and radiated from that center.

You are doing inside exactly what you are doing outside. We were converging the light of the universe, and then we were radiating it out. Now we are converging the all-pervading light, and we are radiating it from the heart center. If what we are saying does not make sense to you, perhaps an illustration of it would be to conceive of a white hole in outer space, through which new energy emerges into this universe from subjacent universes. That is what we meant earlier by saying that we are born anew recurrently—emerging out of the void.

This inner light is different. When you try to define that difference, it is very difficult. The best way is to say that you are talking about the light that sees rather than the light that can be seen. We are not talking about physical light. The only way to strengthen this light is to think of yourself as a being of light, instead of thinking that you are a body that is absorbing light. You are yourself a being of light.

To explore this practice further, you could entertain luminous thoughts, and luminous emotions. Thoughts become luminous when they develop great clarity. The opposite would be ambiguity. If you are not very scrupulous about truthfulness, your thinking will be ambiguous; you are fooling yourself, actually. The more one does the practice of *muhasaba*—confronting your intention, your motivations—the more your thoughts become crisp and clear, rather than ambiguous. The consequence is that you radiate more light.

Whether this has an actual influence on the physical radiance, the bioluminescence, as it is called in biology, or whether we are talking about influencing the radiance of the light that sees rather than the light that can be seen—it is not clear, and it does not really matter, as long as you consciously radiate light.

To pursue this further, we are going to breathe up and down, rather than centripetal/centrifugal. This will help to make us aware of what we call the transcendental dimension. Think of a flame that is rising in your spinal cord as you inhale. And think of all the different colors: red at the bottom of your spine; then a kind of terracotta in the second chakra; orange in the solar plexus; then gold in the heart center; green in the throat center; blue in the eyes; violet in the third eye; and then colorless light at the top of the head.

Instead of just concentrating on this flame rising, represent to yourself the outreach of the flame. Your aura develops a kind of extension, and it becomes rather like several rainbows interspersed with one another: a red rainbow, and then a terracotta rainbow, and then an orange one—and so on. They are interspersing one another. It would be a wonderful challenge for an artist to try to paint this.

Now we encounter a new factor. After transferring your attention from one chakra to the next, you hold your breath. You carry this shift of your attention further into higher planes, but it does not necessarily mean higher in space. Then, when you hold your breath, you make a quantum leap. All of a sudden you cease identifying yourself with your aura and you identify yourself with being pure luminous intelligence.

When you exhale, you experience the impact of intelligence upon your aura. As we have seen, for a hologram to become coherent, and therefore visible, you have to light it up, to illuminate it with a laser beam.

So, imagine that you are lighting up your aura, which is the light that can be seen, with the light that sees, the light of pure intelligence. You experience an outburst of light. Your aura suddenly flares up, simply by the act of awakening.

Now, after practicing awakening, you see that it is a sudden change in perspective. It will give you a jolt, and all of a sudden your whole aura burns more brightly. It flares up suddenly, and you experience its sparkling effulgence.

In the next stage you consciously shape your aura. It would seem, a priori, that you could shape it any way you wish. But, if you started to compose music, for example, you would realize that, although you could compose whatever you wanted, in fact, what you compose does express something of your being. There are forces beyond the purview of your own will or consciousness that take over. This is where in our work, in fashioning our aura, we are going to try to let ourselves be inspired by what we discover as we lift our consciousness into the celestial spheres.

Recall again the plane *malakut*, the plane that you touch upon when you are moved by a need for glorification, a need for the sacred. It triggers off the memory of having been in that celestial condition prior to your birth and your conception.

Try to imagine the countenance—not the contours or the profile, but the countenance—of your face at the level of *malakut*, the level of the angelic plane. Maybe the most popular way of saying this is: "Try to discover your real face." Think that your physical face is a mask. That mask carries a lot of traits, like defenses, disappointments or bitterness. There are a lot of things that have come through owing to your existence or conditions or ancestry.

But your real face is behind this mask. It is beyond your ancestry, beyond the impressions of the world, and irrespective of your parents. It is, you might say, what you are eternally; that is not quite accurate, but still, you could say eternally. It does not really have contours, but if you imagine it as having contours, at least it is a beginning. In reality it is a countenance rather than a face.

It is your emotional attunement that is going to determine that countenance. This countenance changes very quickly. It changes continually, depending upon your attunement. Think of something very beautiful; for example, imagine the angels in the heavens, the great celebration, and the processions and the candles, the light and the music. If you imagine that, and how uplifting it is, your whole face will reflect something of your attunement.

It is true even of your physical face, but your countenance at the level of malakut, the celestial level, is much more malleable than your physical face. It changes much more easily, and lends itself much more readily to the expression of emotion. One of the clues is that it is rather like a child; it is innocent and defenseless. It is not mature.

In a sense, to return to the way we were before we were involved in the process of becoming is a kind of regression. It seems like a regression in time, a regression back into babyhood again. It is only if you can get into the attunement of the child in you that you will grasp the countenance of your celestial body.

There could be some confusion because there are two types of angels. Pir-o-Murshid said there are those who have not incarnated, and those who have resurrected and have returned to that sphere, but who carry with them all the wisdom and maturity that has been gained at the existential level. They do not have the countenance of babies or children anymore; they have the countenance of very wise beings.

So when you try to grasp your celestial countenance, you could either regress in time to try to grasp your pristine state, which is immaculate; or, you could forestall the future. That is, you imagine that the features of the maturity you have gained through your existential life—the wisdom and understanding—are eventually distilled, or transmuted, or sublimated. Then it is not just a wise man or woman, it is more like a master, or, of what we understand by a master.

The know-how that a doctor develops is not useful on the heavenly planes, but the wisdom that the doctor has developed is. The know-how was the underpinning for this wisdom. That wisdom will leave its mark, imprint its mark, upon the countenance of the person who has resurrected.

There you have two images, and you can work with them both. One is the way you were prior to your descent through the spheres; and the other is the way that you will be if you keep on evolving and get transmuted from your present state.

We said that this countenance keeps changing. It would be more true to say that the countenance of the angelic face is not affected by the emotions or attunement of the human level. It is something like a safety buoy that you see at night in the storm: it is only occasionally that you come across it, and then it fades away. You cannot hold it. Yet once you have grasped it, you know. It kind of clicks: you know "This is me." There is no doubt about it. It can be so very different from your physical face, but you know this countenance is much more you than your physical face.

However, it is you in your pristine state. There is that other you that is more like the future in infinite regress, and it is this one that changes according to your attunement. Still, it is just a countenance. It is so rare to catch more than a fleeting glimpse; it seldom gels.

We are going to bring this all much more into focus by working with the confection of our aura. Come back again to the notion of yourself as a being of light, and even the flame rising in the spinal column, and the rainbow.

These are, in a sense, geometrical forms. You can actually mold the effulgence of your aura into a form. It is a very strange thing. Metaphorically, imagine that you are able to mold light with your hands; you are able to give it a form. It will never lend itself totally, but to some extent it is malleable.

Even the physical aura will espouse the contours of the physical body. If you could see your physical aura, you would realize that there are three columns in the middle. The nerve tissue absorbs more light than other forms of tissue, other types of tissue. And the nuclei of your cells absorb more light than the rest of the cell.

So you will find that, indeed, your aura does espouse the contours of your body and your face. It is not absolutely like contours; it does not have a skin. It is like the photographs of Walter Chappell. But notice this: notice how it changes as a consequence of your attunement and of your thought, your realization.

Let us experiment with this. Think of the kind of emotion that you develop if you are mastering a situation—for example, climbing the mountains, or skiing, or conducting a choir. You are exercising mastery. Recollect the emotional attunement that you develop as you are thinking in terms of mastering a situation.

Now you could imagine how your face looks. Notice the difference in your face when you are concentrating on mastery, to the way that your face would look if you were, for example, concentrating on compassion. Keep alternating between these two as a practice. Think of the form of your face when you are exercising mastery. Then think of someone who is suffering, and you feel so sad about that suffering that you would do anything to help. See how the expression on your face has altered, has changed.

That is just the expression of your face. It does not necessarily mean that the profile of your face has changed. But it is an expression that has come through. That is what we are trying to highlight. Identify yourself with the expression, and apply it to your aura: your aura will be configured by your attunement.

So if you are working with mastery, *wali*, the fabric of your aura, which is light, is going to assume the form that expresses mastery. It is not quite as though you were simply fantasizing the confection of a statue, that is, fashioning a statue using your fantasy. This time it is your thinking of the names, thinking of the divine qualities, that is going to determine the form of that statue that you are building out of light. You are converting an attunement into a form. It is the form of your own being.

You will discover that your aura can assume many different forms, whereas your body would offer a lot of resilience in opposition to this formative process. The body, even your face, will not change nearly as much as the countenance of your aura. So you can imagine that your aura will survive the demise of your physical body, just like the light of a star survives the demise of the physical star. We can survive our death, and continue beyond death into what we call resurrection.

These configurations that affect your aura, and also your aura, will keep changing as you concentrate on different qualities. These many-faceted configurations of your aura are distilled further. A concrete way of looking at it would be to imagine that, after the death of your body, your magnetic field continues to live; and, after your magnetic field dies, then the aura continues to live; and so on. The features of your physical body are carried over, but sublimated into your aura. The features of your aura are carried over, and sublimated in your celestial body, at the *malakut* level. So, in some way, you are affecting your celestial body by working with your aura.

Keep thinking of the different qualities. If you are familiar with the Sufi divine names, you can think of the face of truth; and the face of mastery; and the face of compassion; and the face of generosity; and the face of life, being life-giving or life-communicating; and the face of wanting to receive guidance, and so on. Imagine all those different faces, each one corresponding to a different divine name, a different quality. Your aura, the same aura, keeps on changing. Simply by imagining a particular quality you will arouse the emotion corresponding to it and the form triggered off by it.

There is a very controversial theory put forth by Rupert Sheldrake.[2] It has not been demonstrated, but then there are a lot of theories that have not been demonstrated. It took many decades before the Einstein-Podolsky-Rosen experiment was ever demonstrated.[3] So this might be demonstrated one day.

Sheldrake's theory suggests that, if you begin seeding a crystal in a laboratory in New York, and two weeks later in Paris someone starts doing the same thing, the crystal that is being seeded in Paris is going to develop more quickly because another laboratory has already executed the process in New York, even though the laboratories have not communicated with each other. This is due to what he calls the morphogenetic field. Instead of thinking that the template at the *malakut* level, for example, is affecting the formation at the *ajsam* level, he is suggesting that what you are doing at the *ajsam* level is going to affect the *malakut* level.

You can work with the fashioning of the body of resurrection. In other words, we can be what we want to be in the world. Although we do not realize it, all of us know that. But we can also be what we want to be in the future, after death.

---

2 Rupert Sheldrake, *The Rebirth of Nature*, 111. He terms this phenomenon morphic resonance. See also Sheldrake's *A New Science of Life*.
3 See Frithjof Capra, *The Tao of Physics*, 311 ff.

Chapter 9

Applying Meditation to Life

We have explored two awakenings: one beyond life and the other in life; samadhi, and then, awakening in life. We compared it with visiting an architect and seeing the blueprints, or then accompanying the architect and seeing how the blueprints work in practice. Now we will try to build a bridge connecting what we have learned with our life situations.

All of us have problems. Of course, there are different kinds of problems. There are problems about your activity in the world: being successful or not, for example. There are problems in your relationships with people, or at least with certain people. There are problems regarding the degree to which we like or dislike ourselves. And, although we do not always think of labeling it a problem, there is our aspiration to fulfill the purpose of our life. This problematic search to further our spiritual unfoldment can aver itself to be more important than all the others. It just depends upon what we value.

These are problems of different sorts. We are going to study this systematically, starting with a problem concerning your activity in the world. The problem might be: "Well, this situation is really unbearable, but I do not see an alternative." Or it might be: "Yes, I do have a choice, but I would not like to risk it during the recession." Maybe there is not a choice; but if there were a choice, then that would be a problem.

The problems can be very, very tough. For example, the choices faced by parents who have a severely handicapped child; or, accepting the death or the departure of someone you love; or, going through a dark night, when there is nothing to soothe the despair. It could be a feeling of not being appreciated, of not being loved; and then you begin to wonder if there is something wrong with you. So the problem could be your self-esteem. We cannot enumerate all the problems, there are so many.

You may feel that you have a lot of problems. But from among your different problems, select one with which you will work during this meditation exercise. Choose one problem. In view of all that we have learned, see if you can detect a connection between that problem and your own nature, your own idiosyncrasies. Maybe there is one; maybe there is not. But remember the words of Jung: if you do not confront your shadow, it will appear to you in the form of your fate.[1]

Jung saw a relationship between two things where we probably do not see a relationship. Perhaps it is difficult to see. It would be very difficult to accept that we are drawing to ourselves the problems that seem to us fortuitous, or that we ascribe to fate, or even to accident. Jung saw a link there; but there may be cases where there is one, and cases where there is not one.

So, test out whether you can see a relationship in your particular case.

Perhaps it would be too hard on yourself to blame yourself for a situation that seems not to have anything

1 See note 2 in chap. 2.

to do with your character, or situations which seem to be beyond your control. Maybe it would be easier to ask yourself: "Could it be that I am being tested in working with a quality, developing a quality, which is called for in this situation? If so, what is the quality?"

Right away you will say that you cannot limit it to one quality, and you are probably right. So you could earmark a few qualities in which you feel you are being tested. You might find that your selection is arbitrary, and that, in fact, you are tested in all the qualities that you could possibly imagine.

Consider one quality after another of those you have selected. See how, if you would develop this quality in your personality more than you have so far, it would affect the problem. To do this you will have to imagine a real-life situation.

For example, there is a person with whom you are meeting. Imagine that you are more truthful, or more patient—more of whatever the quality is which you are needing to develop. How would your relationship be with that person? How would it alter your conversations, or your handling of your relationship with that person?

As you enumerate several qualities, allow yourself to get into the spirit of each one. The qualities are outlined by the Sufis in what they call *asma ilahi*, the names of God. We call this the *waza'if*, which means "repetition," as with a mantram.

Say, for example, that you imagine yourself being more truthful with this person. You imagine a conversation in which you tell the person how you really feel. There is a chance that it might break the relationship altogether. Do you trust yourself to be able to say it and take that risk—say it politely, of course, but say it?

The questions must also be asked whether you are sparing that person from something that might be hard to hear; and whether it is always, in every case, useful or helpful to spare that person. Your main consideration is, of course, not wanting to hurt. The question is whether you are doing harm by sparing the person.

We find that it is not good enough to work with just one quality. The qualities are sometimes in tandem, some times complementary. For example, along with truth we could consider the complementary quality, which is compassion. Think of that person. If you had more compassion for that person, would it make your relationship easier? Or perhaps you fear that if you did have more compassion, that person would take advantage of your compassion and interpret it as weakness.

So, now you have two qualities in tandem: truthfulness and compassion. You can see whether you can associate those two and be truthful and compassionate at the same time; or whether you can choose one or the other, but you cannot combine the two.

Instead of thinking about the theory involved, think of a definite life situation. Ask yourself very clearly how enhancing these qualities in yourself, and applying them in your relationship to that person, would affect your problem with that person.

Whatever the answer is, we know that if we try to enhance a quality by our will, we will enhance the shadow of that quality. Let us articulate this more precisely. Every quality has its shadow. If you, with your will, try to enhance your truthfulness, you may become simply blunt, and not very subtle.

The shadow of compassion would be permissiveness, or indulgence. So, if you developed more compassion

135

for people, the danger is that you would be too indulgent. As an example, instead of riding your horse, you would let it graze while you are sitting on it. That would be an exaggerated sense of compassion.

In fact, if you want to know what your qualities are, all you have to do is ask yourself what your defects are—because you have the qualities of which your defects are the shadow. If you are lazy, then you are a peaceful person. If you are facetious, then you are a joyous person.

If you are trying to enhance qualities by willing to do so, you will enhance the corresponding defect. Also, there are limits to the extent that willpower can enhance the qualities of your being. But we can do better. Every time that you want to work with a quality, try to reach the quality in its archetypal dimension. See it in its enormous compass. For example, think of the saying of Pir-O-Murshi that he whole of life is a test in which truth triumphs over falsehood.[2]

This is a little bit subtle, but Pir-o-Murshid says it is no use arguing and saying this is the truth; you have to be the truth; and have power but do not use it.[3] Just saying the truth to that person will probably not prove helpful, whereas if they feel that you are a very truthful person, then you are speaking without saying it. That is the more subtle way of accomplishing it. The name here is *haqq,* truth.

In order to enhance this quality in yourself so that you could better deal with your problem, you have to discover truthfulness in your being. You find the qual-

---

2 *The Path of Initiation,* vol. 10, *The Sufi Message of Hazrat Inayat Khan,* 167.
3 *The Inner Life,* 11–12.

ity inherent in your being. That is what Pir-o-Murshid calls our divine inheritance, and it is written right into us. Recognize that it is there in its perfection; also, that you have not always known how to bring it through without just hurting people and making a mess of your life and other people's lives.

We have learned to turn within, to turn inside. The way to apply what we have learned about turning within to this particular problem is to confront our motivations so that we do not deceive ourselves. If we do not deceive ourselves, then we are truthful and other people will feel it. There is no use saying the truth to another person if you are not truthful with yourself.

The same thing is true with any quality you consider, for example, compassion, *rahim*. Instead of trying to see if you can apply more compassion in your treatment of that person, look inside yourself. First of all, acknowledge that in the depth of your being your heart is in tears, if we may put it metaphorically. Acknowledge that you are extremely broken inside as a result of the suffering that you see in the world.

We are living in a hard world, a tough world. You have hardened yourself, because otherwise you find that it leaves you very vulnerable. We are, as the Sufis describe it, like a nut whose shell is very tough yet inside is rather soft. We find difficulty in recognizing the compassion in ourselves, because it would make us feel soft, even mushy; and we find it difficult to apply it to another person.

Once again, it is discovering the qualities in yourself, discovering that they are present in you—in what is called your divine inheritance—that will help you to apply it to people. As a matter of fact, if you have it in you then you do not have to try to be compassionate; your compassion is there, and people will feel it right away. In other words, your relationship with people calls upon you to get in touch with your deeper self.

This is where meditation comes in. If you ask how you can apply meditation to everyday life, that is one of the answers. What we have learned in meditation should help us. We have learned to turn within.

A more pertinent tandem of qualities would be mastery as opposed to listening to your guidance. This is a very useful pair because the quest for mastery, wali, seems to draw us toward outside; and *hadi*, guidance, to turn inside.

So, consider your problem again. Every situation is different, but it might be a case where there is a struggle of wills: that person is trying to dominate you, or you are trying to dominate them. There is a tug of war, of wills, between you. You realize that if you give in, then that person will dominate you, and it will have very serious consequences in terms of your ability to fulfill your objective in life. Unfortunately, that is the way life is.

But, then, what do we mean by mastery? In our mind we associate it with controlling, that is, enforcing our will upon other people. There are a lot of cases of that in the world. If you are called onto that kind of battlefield, then the person who has the strongest ego is going to win.

We are warned by Pir-o-Murshid not to undertake anything that is beyond our ability.[4] Mastery must al-

---

4 See Inayat Khan, *Mastery through Accomplishment*, especially the chapter entitled "Knowledge and Power."

ways in some way be measured by your ability. As you develop more power, you are able to undertake something more challenging.

If you are too foolhardy in your challenge, you can expect to be the loser. That is clearly not the best way of going about it. If you overstress yourself, you lose self-confidence. It is very difficult to reverse that trend. You keep on having to give in, and give in, and give in.

There is another solution. That is, to call upon a power greater than your own power. Consider your will as being like the branch of a tree, and the divine will to be the whole tree. Instead of thinking that your will is a certain will and the divine will is another will, look at it as one tree. Then, somehow, you can call upon a level of your being which you do not limit to your individual ego, and which will give you much more power.

If you have power, other people feel it right away. Pir-o-Murshid illustrated this with an example: if you are playing the piano, are you just using the pressure of your fingers on the keyboard, or is it your wrist, or is it your elbow, or is it your shoulders, or is it the weight of the whole trunk of your body?[5] There are different levels from which you can gain power. If you are using the more individual dimensions of your being, your power is limited, and people soon take advantage of it.

You need to learn how to call upon those wider dimensions of your being. Here again, our meditations should be helpful to you; for example, the meditations in which you grasp the expanse of your being, when your consciousness reaches right out into the stars. There is a sense of immensity in terms of space.

---

5   *The Vision of God and Man*, 120.

Your magnetic field gives you a sense of magnetism; it gives you a sense of strength, energy. If you increase the span of your magnetic field, then it gives you a feeling of having much more strength. Perhaps one of the greatest secrets that we have encountered here is, again, a thought of Pir-o-Murshid Inayat Khan: consider your outreach, your realm of responsibility, upon which you exercise some kind of influence.[6]

What are the meditations for this? We have already come across them. While you are meditating, you consider how circumstances influence you, and how you influence circumstances. You can see how circumstances influence you: you are sad, or glad, or crestfallen, or bucked-up. You can see the influence of the circumstance upon yourself. But your influence upon the environment—we are not talking about control, we are talking about influence—is much more difficult to see.

You know that your thoughts reach other people. Not just that, but you know that people live in you, that people are present in you. That means that those people have an influence on you. When Gandhi died, there was a lady in the suburbs of London, crying. We asked her why she was so sad about Gandhi when there are so many people dying all the time. She replied, "He strengthened my conviction about what is right." Somehow he had an influence on her. So you do have an area of influence upon people, albeit willy-nilly.

Perhaps the whole thing is blown up a little bit saying this, but it is the way that the dervish thinks. There is a saying that the dervish is a king whether in a palace or a hut. It is not the kind of influence that the king has through an army, but a kind of influence through

6 Inayat Khan, *Mastery through Accomplishment*, 232–33.

the outreach of his or her being. There was a dervish named Hazrat Babajan who lived in a modest little hut, but her influence upon people was enormous.[7]

The sense of your impact on the universe will give you a sense of mastery. That is, if you know those areas where your influence is called for, and if you take responsibility to see that these situations are handled properly. In a situation for which you are responsible, you do not allow mistakes to occur without your intervention.

If you are conducting a choir, you never allow a person to sing a false note without responding. You stop right away and say, "Let's do it again." You never allow things to happen out of your control; that is, in areas where you have a responsibility. In other words, taking responsibility is going to increase your power.

That is a deeper sense of the meaning of *wali*. You could perhaps say that *wali* means "taking responsibility." The people who are going to gurus are looking for the guru to take responsibility instead of themselves. Our way is the way of freedom, so we have to learn to take responsibility ourselves. And people feel it right away. They feel here is someone on whom we can count. If you are that kind of person, you will get the job. If the person at that office thinks "I do not know if this person is very reliable," then you will not get the job. That is *wali*.

In its ultimate form, *wali* represents the recognition of the divine power invested in your own being. That is something that does come through in meditation. Perhaps you have noticed, when you have gone very deep in meditation, that you feel endowed with a great power. That is particularly true, for example, after a retreat.

7 See Kevin Shepherd, *A Sufi Matriarch: Hazrat Babajan.*

141

The Sufis distinguish between radiating and encompassing. The area of your outreach, of your influence, is what you encompass. It is often referred to as a kingdom. If you are just radiating, by itself, your energy will get dispersed. Pir-o-Murshid says something which applies in this connection: a very active person has a lot of magnetism, but that magnetism gets dispersed very quickly.[8]

You have to know how to activate the magnetism of your being. However wide its outreach may be, consider it as a zone with a definite threshold or boundary. Do not think of it as a vortex, which has no boundary. Think of your magnetic field in terms of zones. As a matter of fact, if you could sense the magnetic field of people you would realize that there are really quantum leaps: there is a certain zone, and then there seems to be a threshold; and then there is another zone. But it is not linear; it is like quantum leaps in an atom.

So, every day in your meditation, instead of getting into samadhi, review your kingdom. Ask yourself: "Well, how about that person there. I should telephone that person." And: "Yes, I promised that person such-and-such and I did not do it." And so on. People are part of your consciousness.

If you are called upon to be a spiritual guide, then every day in your meditation you have to think of each of the people you are guiding. You might feel that a person is going through a crisis, and that you need to give that person a new practice. That is really taking responsibility for people. It helps you develop *wali*. It gives you *vilayat*: that is the meaning of *vilayat*. It gives

---

8 *Philosophy, Psychology, and Mysticism*, 119.

you mastery, and people feel it right away. You do not have to use a hammer to kill a fly; you can have force and power, but that does not mean you have to use it. A big dog does not have to bark; it is the small dog that barks.

On the other hand, *wali* has to be balanced by *hadi*. In our practices, qualities are usually considered in tandem, otherwise you become pigheaded, as one says; stubborn. You do not want to listen to reason. You are standing on your high horse and do not want to accept that you are wrong. There are a lot of people like that.

Some people think it is demeaning to recognize that they have made a mistake. It is a feature of great beings to recognize their mistakes. In fact, we learn by our mistakes. It is a mechanism written right into our programming, just as, in the replication of the DNA by the RNA, there are enzymes that correct the mistakes in replication—and if they do not, that is when cancer develops.

You have considered how your relationship with that person would change if you are able to call upon the great power in your being. This is done by extending, or expanding, your consciousness; also by reaching upward, and recognizing the divine power as the ground out of which your power arises.

Then you need to work with *hadi*, which is calling upon your intuition. We speak of asking for guidance, but calling upon your intuition is really what it amounts to. It is really not desirable to ask other people for advice, although we do it all the time. It is not taking responsibility; people are only too glad to give you their advice, and they are not always conscious of the very serious consequences their advice can have.

Rather than thinking of that same situation that you have considered thus far, reflect upon a situation in which you really do not know what to do. You really have a need for guidance. If you cannot ask anybody for guidance, how can you find that guidance in your intuition? The trouble is that intuition could be deceptive, it could be just wishful thinking.

Meditation can help you.

If you keep practicing turning within, then you become able to assess how you react to situations, or, as Murshid said, how circumstances affect you.[9] For example, you feel heartened; or you feel discouraged; or you feel upset; or you feel enraged, or outraged—how you are affected by circumstances. So there is a correspondence between inside and outside.

You have already seen that there is a correspondence, but you remember that to turn within you had to give up looking at things in the explicate mode. In the implicate mode, thoughts are jumbled; it is very difficult to see a clear guidance there, a clear indication. It seems a little bit amorphous, nebulous.

You learn to sail in this mist, as it were, and perceive clues that are intermittent and tend to fade away. Let us give an example. During the Second World War, as an officer in the British Navy fighting the Nazis, we were on a minesweeping vessel protecting the forces. We were attacked by U-boats. We were on the bridge in the dark trying to discern, to see if we could see, U-boats in the mist. We were taught, or at least we learned, that if we scanned the horizon we would miss them. We had to have our glance in a state of readiness. The extraordinary thing was that we would feel that

9 *The Alchemy of Happiness*, 169.

submarine; we could feel it in ourself. We did not feel it out there, we felt it inside; and then something called us to look there.

This is an application of what Pir-o-Murshid Inayat Khan said intuition is a revelation of your own spirit.[10] Suppose you are talking to a person, and that person looks you in the eyes and looks very upfront; and then you close your eyes and you feel dishonest. Your intuition is telling you that person is lying, yet nothing in the way of that person gives you any clue that they are lying. This is where meditation would be very helpful.

How do you know whether your intuition is right? Pir-o-Murshid is saying that there is a kind of barometer within you that gives you a sense of the way conditions are outside. But it is very, very delicate, and very fine-tuned. It is only if you have gotten used to turning within that you are able to make any sense of what your inner guidance is saying. Otherwise you are just indulging in wishful thinking, and wishful thinking can be very misleading and even extremely dangerous.

When turning within, we have learned to reach outside from inside. So, for example, to practice *hadi* with this person you would have to try to get into the consciousness of that person. See how it would be if you were that person. That will help you.

Instead of just countering that person with your will in a tug of war, get inside the consciousness of that person. Then you see what the motives are that drive that person. Also, you see the way that person assesses you. You realize that the way they assess you is not the way you assess yourself. You feel that they are mistaken in

---

10 Inayat Khan, *Song of the Prophets*, 139.

their assessment of you, and they are behaving toward you in a way that is not appropriate because their assessment of you is wrong.

Now you realize that you will in some way have to let them know what you feel. You find that, particularly in personal relationships, there is a communications breakdown. The anger that frequently develops creates a situation in which one does not want to hear the other. That is one of the vows that we ask people to make when they are being married: to pledge not to get angry if the other person complains. Then, at least, the lines of communication are open.

You may also find that the person is continuing to assess you the way that you were, perhaps many years ago, and does not realize that you are a new person. That is the reason why Buddha, after his retreat, when his disciples came to him out of curiosity to see what had happened to him, said, "I have attained illumination. Have l ever spoken to you thus before?" He wanted them to know that he was not the same person as he was before. You have got to say it. You have got to come to your partner and say, "I am a new person." And they might say, "Oh, you must have been at a seminar with some weird guru."

In fact, the best conversation between people in a personal relationship is "How do you feel now? Is anything happening to you in your attunement?" "Yes, there are things; there is a realization that I have come to." You have to communicate.

So we have learned to turn within. We were saying that you have to reach outside from inside. Then, at a certain moment, we felt that outside seemed to be rather remote. There might even be a time, for a short while, during which you have to really place a wall between the outside and the inside. Remember that when the sun is in the sky, you cannot see the stars.

In order to see clearly inside, you really have to blank out the outside—or at least the way the outside appears. This is not trying to reach the consciousness of the person from inside. It is trying to find that person in you. The people we know are present in us, in our psyche.

Instead of it being a wall, it could be a buffer. This is illustrated in the Fourth Piano Concerto of Beethoven, where the orchestra, which depicts the world, presents the pianist with a challenge. In his reply, he does not play ball—he responds totally in contrast with the challenge. It is as though he were saying: "I have to consult my deeper self." Beethoven is teaching us a great lesson in meditation.

Consider meditation as a buffer. When you are confronted with a problem, do not react. You call for a halt, a reprieve; and you meditate. When you meditate, you must not keep on dwelling on the problem—that is cogitation, not meditation. Deal with how you feel inside.

Actually, what Beethoven was doing was consulting, accessing, the many-splendored bounty, the resourcefulness, of his being. If you react, it is only the surface of your being that is involved. You are not calling upon all your faculties.

It is important to be clear about this: If he had reacted, that wonderful melody would not have arisen. It is also true to say that if he had not been challenged, it would not have come through either. So you could consider the world as a catalyst that triggers off your resourcefulness.

Sometimes your guidance is simply that a certain quality, or several qualities, are highlighted as you turn within. You do not try to figure this out with your mind: "What are the qualities that I need in order to meet this problem?" Rather, you turn within, and somehow that self-organizing faculty in you highlights certain qualities.

If you are familiar with the language of the names, then you will label these qualities. You will be better able to earmark them if you are familiar with what these qualities are. And then, once more, you can do exactly what we have been doing: recognize that you do have that quality in you. All you have to do then is rely upon it in your action in that particular case.

It is because we doubt whether we have these qualities that we find it difficult to actuate them. Ultimately, it is all a question of faith; not belief, faith—faith in God, as you, in you. That is why Pir-o-Murshid said faith in God is sustained by faith in yourself.[11]

Now let us consider two qualities, again in tandem, that are very close to *wali* and *hadi*: that is, *zahir* and *batin*. There are many meanings to the divine name *zahir*. It means "radiating." Ultimately, it means "the epiphany"; it means that the whole universe is the manifestation of the not-yet-manifest.

Our purpose in life is, therefore, to manifest the non-manifest in our being. Of course, manifestation is very closely linked with radiating. You could radiate light, or you could radiate life, or radiate love, or power. This is again something which you will find helpful in meditation.

---

11 *Sufi Teachings*, 115.

Our radiance gets depleted dealing with the very gross kind of situations we encounter in life. It is very difficult to keep on smiling when everybody is angry or sad; such people do not like your smile. It takes courage to smile. Remember that film of Mozart: it took courage to laugh the way he did to the king.[12]

We are suggesting that, instead of exercising power against that person who tries to dominate you, you radiate a lot of joy and light; it is very much to your advantage. Sometimes if a person counters you with anger and you laugh, it deflects their thrust.

This is where we are challenged: How can we be joyful when life is so hard? It is a great secret. The power of joy is a great secret. You can see the whole universe as an outbreak of joy; spring, the crystals of snow—it is all an expression of joy.

We know that joy is always at the cost of suffering, but we have to transmute our suffering. It is okay to be sad and happy at the same time. Do not think that you cannot be happy because you are sad you can be both. There, again, is something that you develop in meditation.

Working with light, radiating a lot of light, is the most tangible, the most concrete, of all meditation practices. It is something simple that you can do without effort, without any sophistication. All you have to do is represent to yourself the radiance of your aura. Even more effective is working with your glance, working consciously, training yourself everyday to radiate light through your glance.

One way of doing that is to imagine the glance of your two eyes as the beams, the headlamps, of a car. In

12 This refers to a scene in the film *Amadeus*.

a further step, you work with your third eye. You imagine that your third eye is like an x-ray that sees further, or sees more internally, than your eyes.

It is not a matter of seeing; it is a matter of casting a light forward. We generally think of seeing as receptive, whereas this is active. It is very helpful to turn your eyes upward as you inhale, and then forward as you radiate light during the exhalation.

There is a third, further, stage. That is to smile through your eyes. You actually smile through your eyes when you see beauty behind the appearance of things. Imagine looking at a person who is forlorn and broken, and has such a bad self-image, and seeing beauty in that person. When you smile, that person sees their beauty through your eyes. Just imagine what you are doing for that person!

Smiling is much more subtle than laughing. There is a word used by the Sufis: the smiling forehead. Perhaps that is when the third eye is smiling. You know the saying: laugh and the world laughs with you; cry and you cry alone.[13]

That is *zahir*. Now let us consider *batin*.

When you are turned within, you discover such bounty that you feel you would be betraying a trust if you were to try to translate it into words. You feel you would expose it to derision and sacrilege. There is a sense of safeguarding something very sacred in yourself, and revealing it only in so far as it feels prudent to do so. You reveal it to those who are ready.

Then you realize that the whole view of the Sufis is that God is continually revealing or concealing the Divine Being depending upon the ability of people to

13 See Ella Wheeler Wilcox, "Solitude."

handle the power of that revelation. We are being protected from the power of the reality behind the surface
of things by maya, by the appearance, by the illusion.
That is our protection, according to the Sufis.

But be conscious of the power of the sacredness in
the depth of your being. You do not have to reveal it.
You reveal it in the measure in which people can deal
with it. But it needs to be safeguarded, and by revealing
it you do incur the danger of exposing it to sacrilege.

This is something which is enacted in the Catholic
Mass: People having gone to take the holy sacrament
at the altar come back to their seat, and you can see by
the way that they walk and by their whole atmosphere
that they feel as though they are carrying something
very sacred in their being. Behind this ritual of some
kind of biscuit that the people are eating is the sense
of participating in the sacredness of God and having
to protect it.

Perhaps one of our greatest needs is to have a sense of
the sacredness that is invested in our being. This knowledge protects us from being wayward and defiled. That
is the meaning of *batin*.

Recognizing the sacredness of your being gives you
a power that confounds those who only know how to
use their will. That is what Jesus had when confronting
Pilate. Pilate did not know how to deal with the being
of Jesus; he washed his hands.[14] If you find yourself at
loggerheads with a person who is using their ego, and
you do not have that kind of gruff ego to counter them,
you can call upon this spiritual power which comes out
of recognizing the sacredness in your being.

---

14 Matthew 27:24.

Chapter 9

Think of yourself as a temple. This is exemplified by a woman who was being lynched by a mob in the South, and she said, "You can do what you like with my body, but you cannot touch my soul." That gives you a very great inner power. You do not have to use external means to counter those who are trying to dominate you; you would be losing anyway. But they cannot meet you where you are strong.

The practices that will enhance this quality are the zikr, which, through its motion of circumambulating the heart, is essentially building a temple; and any practice of glorification, such as 'azim, or 'ali or 'aziz—that is, whenever you are calling upon sacred emotions instead of the personal emotions of anger, or joy, or satisfaction, or selfishness.

This sacredness is also the reason for silence in a retreat. But the outer observance does not quite do it. What Ibn 'Arabi calls the silence of the heart is much more important. You are always conscious of this sacred core of your being, even in an ice-cream parlor or a supermarket.

The objective is to be able to hold this awareness, not just in your meditation when, of course, you can reach it, but in everyday life. You do not have to go to church, you do not even have to meditate—as long as you are able to maintain that consciousness of the sacred within your being. It will preserve you from slipping into vulgar emotions.

You become sensitive to the kind of emotions that people emit. As Pir-o-Murshid said, "You can see the degree of evolution of a person by noticing what makes them laugh and what makes them cry."[15] You become

15 Inayat Khan, unpublished paper. See also *The Awakening of the Human Spirit*, 186.

very sensitive to the emotional attunement of people, and you safeguard your emotional attunement. In fact, you see the kind of influence that people exercise upon your attunement, and you realize how easy it is to slip into low key, or even vulgar, emotions.

This does not mean being sanctimonious. It simply means that you have a sense of dignity. But it is true that in this place you are lonely.

Everyone needs space, however much you like to share and communicate with other people. It makes for happier relationships with people if a person respects the sacred space of others. As stated by Kahlil Gibran, Great trees do not grow in each other's shadow.[16]

Putting aside in your daily life a time to meditate will set a boundary in your personal relationships. It will make it clear that this is that space, this is the sacred space that I need. If you do not have this space, you become out of sorts, and cantankerous, and angry—because you have this need, and this need needs to be respected.

In your relationship with a person, it could be that this person tends to try to get power over you by ridiculing your sense of the sacred. In fact, that is what is happening everywhere in the world. It is what you call sacrilege. That is where you can definitely counter by saying: "This is my business," or "This is my area." If people ask inquisitive questions, you do not have to answer them; you owe your allegiance to God.

So that is *batin*, the veiled one. The veil is a protection, but, as the Sufis say, the veil both conceals and reveals

---

16 Kahlil Gibran, *The Prophet*, 17. "And stand together, yet not too near together: / For the pillars of the temple stand apart, / And the oak tree and the cypress grow not in each other's shadow."

the face. It espouses the contours of the face. The veil is permeable, but it gives you some screening, some ability to reveal what you feel is okay, and to conceal that which you feel needs to be protected.

There is a further development of this because, obviously, *batin* does stand for turning within. As we have already encountered, when we turn within we discover the digestion of the psyche. The psyche is digesting the influence of the environment, and you feel it in your solar plexus.

In fact, in cancer patients there is a shortage of a hormone in the pancreas because the pancreas is overstressed. At the physical level, the pancreas can be overstressed by eating too many proteins and not being able to break the amino acid chains and reconstruct them.

In the same way, the psyche can be overstressed. You feel it in the solar plexus, because that is where we turn within. If you remember, when we turn within the solar plexus it is the threshold that gives you access to inside. That is where this feeling of *batin* may give you the sense that you have need of protection.

There is a divine name for that: *muhaymin*; that is, asking for further protection. Your defenses are saying: "I do not want my privacy to be encroached." Yet perhaps, out of compassion or kindness, you allow this to happen because you will be hurting a person by turning them away. Then you are the one who registers the damage.

So in meditation we learn how to deal with problems. We learn to discover in ourselves the means of dealing with them. Think of your problems again, now in the light of the few qualities that we have discussed. There are many, many other qualities, but we have considered enough to indicate the method to pursue.

Let the power of joy pervade your soul and lift you above the tribulations of your life with a sense of ease. In the last resort it will be all right. A defeat can aver itself to be a victory. Going through the darkness you reach into the light. Suffering will open the way to the exaltation of joy.

Chapter 10

Wazifa

We have come to a point at which we want more practical indications about how to work. We need to answer the question: What is the role of the repetition of a divine name in our practices? Why are we repeating the divine name?

To state it very simply, the sound helps to bring the thought into focus. If you think of all the explanations that we have given about a few different names, you might wonder whether you could remember all of those explanations when you are repeating the name. Through repetition, the meaning of the name becomes implicit in your understanding. The name is like a label or a sign of recognition, a reference in your mind's index system.

In the Sufi tradition, we are using Arabic words, whereas in Hindu practice Sanskrit words are used. That is not very important. The beauty is that you are using a word that is not in your ordinary dictionary. It does not have the limitations that you ascribe to words in your own language. That is why scientists sometimes use Greek words, or Greek letters, as references.

We must not discount the fact that the sounds them-selves do convey something of the attunement of the name. When you hear the sound, you can ascertain yourself how the sound conveys the meaning. The important thing is the association between the sound and the meaning. That is what our language is about. We are continually associating the meaning and the sound. By the process of association, the sound will immediately evoke the meaning.

The beauty of the repetition is that you are training the unconscious. You are instilling a thought form, a seed thought, in the unconscious at the archetypal level. We could even say it wears pathways in your brain, so that the thought pops up into the conscious from the unconscious when called upon.

As an example, imagine you have been invited to a party. You ask who is coming, and are told so-and-so and so-and-so; and then there is a name, and you think "Oh no, if that person comes, I am not coming." But you remember having said the name *rahman* (compassion), and so you say, "Yes, okay." Somehow you have built something in your unconscious, and somehow it has registered there. It has a label. Rahman has a meaning for you that the word "compassion" does not have. It has gained a meaning by all that you have put into it.

The divine names are effective just by dint of the power of training the unconscious. There are other dimensions of divine names that make them more effective; in fact, much more effective. You could, for instance, consider a name as an attunement, rather than a thought that can be translated as a word. We are a bit wary of descriptions of the names translated into English because then you tend to reduce a name to the meaning of that word. It is much better to think of each divine name as an attunement. Then you understand the role of the sound much better, because the sound conveys an emotional attunement far beyond what the words could ever convey. There is a kind of magic in it.

Behind all of this there are more general laws. Every object in the world has its signature tune, whether it is a piece of paper, or whether it is a gong, or whether it is the atoms of our body. Everything has its frequency range, and that is known as the language of the universe. Scientifically it is called the audiosphere. It was Pythagoras who said if you could hear the symphony of the spheres, it would give you access into the meaning behind the universe.[1]

Proclus, a Neoplatonic philosopher who lived in the fifth century, went further: "If you could hear the sound that is produced by the heliotrope [that is, the sunflower], as it keeps on turning its head toward the sun, the friction between the flower and the air; and if you could hear the sound produced by the planets in their whirling; and if you could hear the sound produced by the stars, [and today we would say the galaxies], you would hear the symphony of the spheres; and you would realize that this symphony is based upon a basic harmony, the harmony of the spheres."[2]

Today, scientists are questioning whether the origin, the original state, of the universe is a harmonious state. The chaos theories propose it begins with chaos rather

---

1 Pythagoras (582–507 B.C.E.) was an influential Greek philosopher, mathematician, and spiritual teacher.
2 "The Prayer of the Heliotrope," https://www.hamilton-landmarks.org/goulish/. Proclus (410–485) was a Greek philosopher. In addition to his own writings, Proclus is credited with organizing the teachings of Plotinus into *The Enneads*.

than orderliness. But we could say that the stage at which we are now encompassing the universe—at this stage, there is a lot of entropy. We have lost sight of the original harmony.

We can also say that the original harmony was embryonic: it gains richness by having passed through entropy. Prigogine's theories state that creativity is always born out of a breakdown of an order replaced by a new order.

So we would say that behind all that we are doing with the *wazifa*, the sound is tuning us to the symphony of the spheres. Just by selecting a particular note in that symphony we are establishing some kind of connection.

When you are repeating a divine name, you can think that you are attuning yourself. In the sound of your voice you have a wonderful feedback system. If you are sensitive to music, you will be able to immediately ascertain whether the sound of your voice is or is not conveying the quality within your being that you are trying to unfold through the name.

You continually correct the way you say the name, just like a musician is continually correcting his or her execution of music. Pablo Casals would stop all the time. He would start playing, and after two or three notes he would stop; he would growl, and then try it again. He would do it again, and again, and again; he would never be satisfied.

Just repeating a name thirty-three times, or one hundred and one times, does not do it. You have to stop, try it again, admonish yourself: that is not good, try it again. Eventually you will find that, by bringing in the right intonation, you will correct your assessment of that quality. You will learn something about that quality through the feedback loop.

This requires of you a very high sensitivity toward music and sound in general. This sensitivity is what the great musicians in India used to develop. Maula Bakhsh, for example, used to play the rudra vina eighteen hours per day. He was continually tuning his soul.[3] That is the reason Indian musicians take such a long time to tune their instruments: the instrument is just a feedback system that enables them to tune their soul.

By repeating a divine name, you get into a certain attunement. But this does not happen quickly. Repeating a name thirty-three times because it has been prescribed does not build the attunement. It would be good to make a retreat in which you could go into it more deeply. There is always the danger of automation, which happens when you do not stop and correct yourself. If you are playing the piano, and you just go on playing without correcting yourself, then you will never improve. It is the same with the *wazifa*.

This is something you can do: even if you just say the name three times, then stop and listen to the reverberation, or the echo. Listen in. The fact is that every atom, every molecule of the ambient air and the walls, and even of the ether of space, each neutrino, is going to pick up the vibrations that you are producing and send them back to you. It is just like radar—they boomerang the vibrations back to you. You might not hear them, but there you have a wonderful feedback system.

It is not just reverberating back to you the sound that you sent out: it communicates a message to you in the way in which it sends your voice back to you. The

3 Maula Bakhsh (1833–96) was a well-known Indian musician and Hazrat Inayat Khan's grandfather, in whose house and atmosphere Inayat was raised.

sound has been altered by whatever way the universe is responding to the messages that you are sending out to it. It becomes a dialogue with the universe.

You can imagine, now, how people are totally trans-figured by the divine name. There are teachers, such as Sant Kirpal Singh, who do not believe in using man-trams or names The reason is, according to Singh, be-cause you are limiting the sound that you tune into by the sound that you send out. This is true. But, on the other hand, by sending a sound out you get a response.

There is another aspect of this, which is a reason for concern. Exactly as, if you press your fingers on your cornea, you have an optical illusion of light, if you press closed the flaps of your ears with your thumbs and listen for the sounds of the inner world, rather than the sounds of the outer world, you will be hear-ing the buzzing of the fluid in your semicircular canals. You will think that you are listening to the sounds of the universe. You are fooling yourself.

However, there is a Catch-22 here.[4] The Brownian movement of the molecules in the fluid of the semicir-cular canals of your ears is somehow connected with the harmony of the universe. It communicates that harmony to you in a personalized way. This happens if you are not trying to listen to sound, but you are using sound as a trigger to get in touch with the symphony of the spheres. That is exactly what Pir-o-Murshid says about the practice called *shagal*: the light that you see or you think you see is simply the trigger that awakens in

4 *Catch-22* is the title of a novel by Joseph Heller, published in 1961. In common usage the phrase refers to a situation in which whatever course of action is chosen leads to an objection or an entrapment.

you the awareness of the light of the universe.[5] That is a way to avoid fooling yourself when repeating a name.

There are many more aspects of this. You could consider each divine name as the signature tune of an angel. So you are communicating with beings instead of just entertaining abstract thoughts. This takes away the mind-trip of the name.

You imagine that the angels embody qualities—that is exactly what we have been working with, embodying qualities—even in the features of their countenance. Imagine what the features of the archangel Wali would be. You could imagine the archangel Michael, for example. Or, what would be the features of the archangel of realization? That would be the archangel Gabriel.

This would be one way of working. It is something that will lift you above the drudge of trying to develop a quality in yourself. That is perhaps the worst thing you can do: repeating a divine name, thinking, "I want to develop this quality." It does not work that way. You cannot be creative trying to be creative. The only way to be creative is to be moved, to be shattered to the core of your being, so that you cannot not write what is coming through. You get up in the middle of the night and you have to write.

It should be so, when you are working with a name, that name continues to function in your mind even while you are sleeping. In fact, it is very good to fall asleep while you are meditating because then your meditation continues in your sleep. Then you might come to a point when you capture a thought that has been triggered off by the name, and you get up quickly

---

5 Inayat Khan, unpublished manuscript.

to write it down. The name serves to trigger off realizations.

There are certain realizations that click at a certain moment; suddenly you see it. Those are important moments in your life. If you do not try to make use of that gift, of what is called the divine revelation, then it will be lost. That is the reason to try to capture it while it is happening. It is very useful to write it down. The name continues to work beyond the moment when you are repeating it, so any time of the day these thoughts might germinate. You need to meditate on those thoughts generated by the name. Then the divine name is really very effective.

The other thing is getting in touch with teachers, or prophets, or saints, who epitomize this particular quality. All of them epitomize all qualities, but you tend to see in each of them a particular quality. In Shiva one sees mastery; and in Christ, *rahman*; and in the Virgin Mary, purity, or the immaculate state; in Abraham, sovereignty. You will find it easier to understand the name if you can think of a being who embodies it, instead of thinking of it in the abstract.

We learn, in the Sufi tradition, to get into the consciousness of a teacher who epitomizes the quality for you when you are repeating the name. When you are saying *qahir*, for example, get into the consciousness of Abraham. If you do this, you will say *qahir* very differently from the way you would say it from your own vantage point.

That is the way of discovering your divine inheritance. You somehow ascribe to the teacher the same quality which you have in yourself, but in a more perfect measure. You do have the quality in yourself, but you do not see it. It is easier to see it in the master—that is, in the teacher, or the saint, or the prophet.

The most important feature of the *wazifa* is making a pledge. For example, if you say the name *wali*, you have to make a pledge that you are going to overcome addictions. You just have to figure out which is your worst addiction: that is where you work. If it is *haqq*, you have to make a pledge that you are never going to tell a lie.

It is the way of the knight, not the way of the monk. That which makes the knight is a pledge. That is the meaning of *bayat*. Initiation in the Sufi Order is a pledge.[6] That pledge is to serve the spiritual hierarchy of the government of the world.

The further aspect of the *wazifa* is working with the form of your celestial body, with structuring, or configuring, your subtle body. It makes the name much more effective if it is sustained by a concrete representation of the form that your subtle body would assume when it is attuned to that particular quality.

You might think, " Well, this is just imagination." The Tibetans work with representations of divinities which are very stylized. Sufis are much more free, because we can imagine the form that we want. The Tibetans use a very definite statue as a figurative representation of a deity. The deity is, of course, always the representation of a certain principle, just like our divine name.

By meditating on that form they shape their etheric body, they fashion it, to such an extent that when they walk in the street they think they are that deity. You might think that is the very essence of mental derangement, but actually there is a great power in it.

6 The Sufi Order is now known as the Inayati Order.

You discover that you are all beings. You discover the many-faceted aspects of your being instead of limiting yourself to your self-image.

The art of an actor is to discover roles that are already latent within, instead of thinking one is playing the role of another person, that one is merely role-playing. You are discovering roles in your being that are latent. It is very, very powerful. What the Tibetans say is that people do not see that you have changed because they judge you from your face—except those who have eyes to see. But eventually it will begin to manifest in your outer body. If nowhere else, it will show to some extent in the features of your face, and in your way of walking, or of sitting. Your movements convey something of what is happening inside you.

There is one aspect of this that we left out earlier. We were working with discovering our angelic countenance in its pristine state. We were anticipating resurrection, by reaching up to the *malakut* level. We have been working with fashioning the aura. There is something a little more difficult to understand which is, again, epitomized by the voice of Caruso in its distortion. That is, instead of thinking that you are fashioning your aura, imagine that you are discovering something that is already there. It is just like discovering the voice of Caruso within its distortions. Plotinus said that the sculptor is unveiling the form that is already in the wood.

So you are not really fashioning your body of resurrection, although you think that you are. You feel that you are creating, but that which appears to be created is a reality being discovered. That is the guarantee that it is not fantasy. There is a difference between creativity and fantasy; there is congruence in creativity, whereas fantasy could be anything. A little dash of this color, and another color, and it is worth $10,000, because it is an important painter; it is pure fantasy.

You cannot change a note of the music of Bach; it is not fantasy. The word for that is "integrity": the integrity of a work of art. Actually, it is a congruence; it makes sense. The artist has crystallized the meaning of the universe into a form. It is a very important thing, because that is what the whole universe is about: it is all about the way in which meaningfulness is coagulated into form.

That gives you something very concrete to work with in your meditation.

Chapter 11

Sound and Vibration

In our meditations, we have been using different methods to train ourselves. We were working with the aura. Besides the aura, we have an *akashic* body. This is more difficult to define. It is something like the frequency range of a gong. There are potentialities, thresholds between which frequencies the gong will begin vibrating. It has an ability to resonate in sympathetic resonance with the sound that it hears.

There has been a scientific exploration that demonstrates that sound is a source of energy. People who are deprived of sound get into a very lethargic state. That is why music is a very important element in meditation. The Chishti Sufis use music. The monks use music to attune themselves. Because of this need of the monks to attune themselves to a celestial pitch, much of the beautiful music of our heritage has come to be.

In meditation, we want to reach a high degree of awareness. Consequently, we will be able to rebirth ourselves by combining, or integrating, the different components of our being into a new unit. That is what we are: we are hybrid. We need to be very clear about the elements that have come together in the formation of our being, and, in the fourth stage of the alchemical process, recombine them anew.[1] As a consequence, we become a new person.

The rishis sit in the Himalayas listening to the cosmos. Of course, Shiva played the rudra vina; actually, he invented the rudra vina, made out of the gourds and animal guts and horns of animals that he could find. But the sound produced by the instrument was just a trigger intended to get the listener in touch with the music of the spheres.

It is not a question of listening to it but of listening in: finding in yourself a vibration that is in resonance with what you are picking up from the universe.

In our meditations we try to explore the enormous expanse out of which we are born, the enormous bounty that has converged into our being. You will find, you will recognize, two elements. On the one hand, you will be aware of the tremendous storms in outer space, the clashes of the galaxies; the stardust, the whirling, the torment, and the gestation leading to the birth of Planet Earth, and, eventually, your birth. All of that is incorporated somehow in your being. Then, if you let your consciousness be raised high, you will find yourself attuned with the music of the angels. We are born out of the admixture of these two components of our being. That is the alchemical marriage.

So, we propose a meditation in which we extend our consciousness right into the stars in the galaxies. You will find that the kind of music which communicates

---

1 The fourth stage of the alchemical process is the marriage, which is the central symbol of alchemy. See Titus Burckhardt, *Alchemy*, 149 ff. Stage four marks the reemergence of spirit from the immaculate state into life.

this aspect is lacking in compassion. It is lacking in humor. There are many things that have developed in the human being but which are not found in the primeval state of the universe. You will, however, find a source of enormous power and grandness. It will give you a sense of the immensity of your being. On the other hand, if you allow your consciousness to be attuned to the higher spheres, then you will discover in yourself something of the nature of the celestial beings.

Combining these two is the great art of life. Remember these words of Pir-o-Murshid: God can attain a great degree of perfection in a human being, but where human beings participate consciously in their creativity, God can attain a higher degree of perfection.[2] We are trying to consciously grasp the elements composing our being, and consciously intermesh them into a beautiful composition.

The first meditation that we suggest is that you are right out there doing a space walk in outer space. Simply identify yourself with your aura; and when you are looking at the stars, you realize that the stars, and even the whole universe, are luminous. The stars are just points in the universe where the light of the universe has been centered. You realize that your aura is made of the light of the stars, and that your aura spreads out into the starry sky. You are not the observer anymore, observing other than yourself; you discover being a part of the cosmos without any boundary.

To help you do this, you could listen to music that seems to tell you something about your primitive roots. For an example, listen to the Symphony of Psalms by

---

2 *The Inner Life*, 325.

Stravinsky. There is no compassion in it; there is no love. There is a struggle. You feel something of the motion of the stars, a kind of geometrical harmony. It sends your consciousness right out beyond the planet. You can see that the planet is emerging out of that incredible choreography of the galaxies.

If you lift your consciousness just a little bit higher, you will hear the overtones rather than just the gross sounds. Overtones serve as a kind of ladder that helps your consciousness lift itself. Imagine that, indeed, if you listen to the symphony of the spheres by attuning yourself to a higher pitch than the lowest common denominator, then you will begin to hear, you will begin to grasp, a richness that you did not hear in the primitive sounds of the universe.

We do not have to think that the universe is just physical—fossilized matter. We can be aware that there is a reality out there that is pure sound, and that we belong to that reality. These vibrations have the faculty of awakening corresponding vibrations within us. That is, of awakening the chakras, which then start vibrating. It is exactly what happens if you have two gongs in the room and one gong has some frequencies in common with the other. If you play one gong, then the second one will start vibrating.

Each sound corresponds with a frequency within your own akashic body, and listening to it causes the corresponding vibration to awaken. You might also notice that the lower sounds seem to affect your lower chakras, and the higher sounds affect the higher chakras. Vibrations are a source of energy. They awaken factors in your being which were dormant.

Accomplished musicians have a very great sensitivity about the way that vibrations affect a human being. When your quest for glorification is sustained by musical sensitivity, then you are capable of producing great works of art. A great work of art evidences the evolution taking place in the universe. It is the impending sense of God, of the reality of which these planets are just the body, that spurs the evolutionary advance further and further afield.

It is as though there is a kind of intuition that reality is many-tiered, that it exists on several levels. We have the faculty, as humans, of grasping something of the higher levels of that many-tiered reality. By grasping it we attune ourselves to it, and we discover aspects of our being that would have remained latent if we had not been able to follow our intuition about the splendor that transpires behind the universe.

What we are trying to do is to enact on the earth plane something of our intuition of the great celebrations in the heavens. We find that it is by following this intuition that we are able to raise ourselves above our despair and sadness. We do have in us, in what we are calling our akashic body, frequency ranges that give us access to the heavenly spheres. You will find that there is some level of your being that is able to sing with the angels. You can sing it—your soul can sing it, even if your voice cannot. In so doing, you are participating in the cosmic celebration in the heavens.

To recreate ourselves, we need to integrate these two poles of our being. You can see that the more primitive pole, the underpinning, needed to be infused with the joy of the heavens to evolve—something like the yeast in making bread. Perhaps we can recognize these two elements in ourselves, and see how our longing for our highest ideal has the effect of transforming the gross matter of our being. It ennobles us.

We are attuning our emotions. If we become highly sensitized, then we cannot brook vulgar or gross emotions. This emotional attunement is a governing factor in our rebirthing.

We see that there are aspects of ourselves that are not in line with our highest aspirations. By attuning ourselves to the higher attunements, those aspects of us that are not in tune tend to drop away. They do not have a place in our attunement. That is why Pir-o-Murshid said: those qualities that one is not attached to will fade away.[3] You do not have to fight them. It is a question of withdrawing your interest in them, your attachment to them.

---

3 *The Alchemy of Happiness*, 174–80.

Chapter 12

The Instant of Time

There is a practice, a breathing practice, which promotes a sense of balance.[1] It is very good to do it in the morning. You inhale alternately through the left and right nostrils, and then, afterward, through both nostrils. You will find that it puts you in balance again after any disturbing dreams you might have. It is like setting the clock for the day.

It is very simple, of course; but if you start introducing thinking into the practice then it becomes a little more sophisticated. Actually, you are balancing left and right, and top and bottom, as if based on the cross. You are calibrating your life-field; first polarizing it by segregating the poles and, consequently, being able to calibrate it.

Place the thumb of your right hand under your chin, and the middle finger of your right hand in the proximity of your right nostril. Then place the palm of your left hand on the back of your right hand, with the thumb of your left hand in the proximity of your left nostril.

---

1 This book is the record of a carefully guided collective spiritual retreat, and that the practices described in this chapter should not be taken up outside the context of guided training in the Esoteric School of the Inayati Order.

Exhale through both nostrils, and keep exhaling as long as you can. Always exhale heavily through both nostrils before you start. Then press your right finger to close the right nostril, and inhale through the left nostril. Think of lifting your energy up the spine, transmuting it as it rises. Press the left finger so that both nostrils are closed. Turn your eyeballs upward and hold your breath. Exhale through the right nostril, bringing the energy down.

Now breathe in through the right nostril, drawing energy up through the right trunk of the spinal cord; hold your breath, with eyeballs turned upward; then exhale through the left nostril, bringing the energy down. Then breathe in through both nostrils, with the energy rising in the spine; hold the breath, turn the eyeballs upward; and exhale through both nostrils as you descend.

Let us reflect on what we are doing in this practice, which is known as *qasab*. There are three channels in the spinal cord. There is the central one that runs inside the spinal cord, and there are two lateral passages, left and right. The lateral channels govern the autonomic nervous system; the central one governs the central nervous system. These two systems are connected by the afferent and efferent nerves.

First, by mind over body, by your concentration, you are able to enhance the flow of energy upward in the left channel of the spinal cord. Then, when you hold your breath, you are dealing with a totally different kind of energy, which we like to call celestial energy. When you exhale through the right nostril, you are bringing that very fine energy down—at least in your mind, you are bringing it down—along the right trunk of the spinal cord.

Then, as you breathe in through the right nostril, you are drawing earth energy upward, and transmuting it as it moves up the right channel of the spinal cord. As you hold your breath, you attune to pure spirit, celestial energy. Then, as you exhale, you infuse your whole magnetic field with the power of pure spirit, which is descending through the left channel.

This interplay with celestial energy is particularly important as you breathe in through both nostrils, because then you concentrate on the central channel. Telluric energy, earth energy, is drawn upward; and at that moment it is important to be conscious of each chakra. You need to be familiar with each chakra, and as the energy passes through the chakra it seems to light up just like a bulb. You are not just shifting energy upward; you are also transmuting the energy. The higher chakras are very sensitive, and they get damaged by earth energy unless it is transmuted and refined.

All that you have learned about lifting yourself beyond your earthly condition is going to help you attune yourself, when you hold your breath, to pure spirit. We call this immaculate condition *quddus*. When you exhale, you infuse your whole magnetic field with the power of pure spirit. It is a sense of being permeated by and infused with this very fine, very beautiful energy.

You have already learned to continue the voyage upward after holding your breath. The thrust that you have set into motion as you transferred your attention from one chakra to the next continues to carry you further while you hold your breath. As we have already said, Pegasus can not go any further. Bellerophon has to continue to pursue the quest on the momentum that has been imprinted upon him by Pegasus.

175

Remember the planes that we explored earlier. For each level of energy, each plane, there is a level of mind. The level of mind corresponding to *ajsam*, the subtle body, is the realm of creative mind; it is distinguished from the gross mind, which corresponds to the energy of the physical body. Then, *mithal*: your mind is now thinking in terms of metaphors, and you are encouraging, or fostering, the creative imagination.

The next stage is *malakut*, in which we tried to highlight our celestial countenance. There is still some kind of formative process taking place at this level. Although the form does not have a contour, the configuration does give you some sense of your real being. You feel that your physical face is a mask.

The next level is beyond thinking. It is the realization of the splendor beyond the universe. That is the plane *jabarut*. Beyond it, we reached up to *lahut*, which is the plane of the archetypes, the divine names, the divine perfection. Then, ultimately, *hahut*, which is unity.

If you are familiar with these planes, and remind yourself of them while doing this exercise, the practice will be more fulfilling than just doing the breathing.

It is also good to remember the first practice that we described. As you exhaled, you were experiencing the divine nostalgia coming through you as your desire to build a beautiful world of beautiful people. And, when you inhaled, you felt the divine freedom, whereby you were able to extract the quintessence of your know-how into what you might call wisdom. This is then integrated, or recycled, back into the software of the universe. If you remember this, it will make *qasab* much richer than just doing the breathing practice.

There are further aspects of it. You could represent to yourself that you are a vortex. You know that the center of a vortex is a vacuum. If you are very sensitive, as you do this practice you will feel the energy of the two lateral channels tending to be drawn into the central channel.

This is a yogic practice. The yogis do it because they are trying to ensure the sovereignty of the central nervous system over the autonomic. It is the way of mastery. There is no function, no autonomic function, that does not fall under the control of the will. You are encouraging the flow of energy from one system to another, from the lateral channels to the central one, through the efferent nerves. So you will feel that pull toward the center; it is a kind of suction effect.

The energy that is rising from the earth is rising and being drawn inward at the same time. You could say that we are conjoining the practice of turning within and the practice of lifting our consciousness upward—both at the same time. We have been practicing these separately, and now they come together.

When you exhale, you experience the opposite: the energy of the central system gets diffused in the lateral channels. That is where the central nervous system is able to exercise governance over the autonomic system. You feel the energy of pure spirit descending in the central channel, and it keeps bifurcating left and right.

If you are very sensitive, you will realize that as you breathe in through the left nostril and draw earth energy upward, it is going to be drawn to the left. And because there is a suction effect in the center, it will rise as a spiral. It will whirl around the vacuum in the center, moving in a clockwise direction. As you exhale through the right nostril, then the energy is going to flow down clockwise also. If you breath in through the right nostril, the energy will spiral upward in the opposite direction, that is, counterclockwise.

As you breathe in through both nostrils, these spirals crisscross at the front of the second chakra; the back of the solar plexus; the front of the heart center; the back of the throat center; and the front of the third eye. They meet at the top of your head. If you advance further, then you will realize that, in fact, the spirals double-loop at each chakra; it is just a little more difficult to feel how the energy hits both the front and back of each chakra as it rises.

So by the power of your imagination you can set the currents in your magnetic field into motion; consequently, you will be energized. You will find that it makes all the difference in your day. It is advisable to do this practice every day.

At first it seemed there was a polarization up and down, and also left and right. Then we found that there was a polarization up and down, but also centripetal/centrifugal. Let us look at this again—the left and right forces. You will find that the model of the pendulum will help you to understand what is happening to you.

The pendulum swings from the extreme point of its swing to the left, to the extreme point on the right. The velocity increases in the course of the swing, and peaks in the middle of the swing; then it decreases, and reaches zero when the pendulum has reached the extreme end. You could say that it has, before it swings back in the opposite direction, experienced a state where time stands still. You could think that not only space is landscaped by gravity, but time, also. Time can go quite fast, and slow down, and even stop.

The situation where time has been suspended is an extremely important one. It is a condition of precarious equilibrium. If you know something about Prigogine's theories, you know that creativity is always a fluctuation from a precarious equilibrium. That is when you can most easily bring about a change.

The easiest point at which to influence the course of the swing of the pendulum is at that moment when it is at rest. When the energy is stronger, it is more difficult to involve. That is the whole secret of the scalar level, the level where the magnetic force has been neutralized by solenoids. You are able then to influence the flow of electrons by using very, very little force.

Perhaps you know that the most favorable time to bring about a change in your life is in a crisis situation. When things are going smoothly, you tend not to change your life. When things are breaking down, that is when a real change is possible. The breakdown is written right into the programming of life. Take advantage of it.

A decision is taken in the instant of time. It takes time to dither, but once you have made a decision, it clicks—it happens in the instant of time. The dervishes attach a lot of importance to the instant of time, and they clearly distinguish the instant of time from the moment of time. In the moment of time, the past overlaps the future. For an example, imagine you are listening to music; the notes you have been hearing continue to resonate in your ears as you hear the next note—there is an overlap. Or, simply consider that at this moment the past is still sort of present in your mind; and you are already forestalling the future.

But the program of the universe provides us with a situation which you could call an apostrophe, when there is a sudden break, a sudden change. You could say a quantum leap. Life is not linear; it is granulated. There are phases, and, as a matter of fact, in the laws of physics, there are forbidden zones. For example, a planet cannot be anywhere between its orbit and the orbit of another planet; otherwise they would collide. This is on the basis of quantum physics. You find it also in music, where there is such a thing as an apostrophe before the last note.

You are breathing in through the left nostril, and breathing out through the right. You have a sense of being drawn into the process of becoming.

We always think of causality as being a flow from left to right. Even in countries where the residents write from right to left, time is represented as moving from left to right. Newtonian physics was based upon this Laplacian theory of causality, which is now being questioned in science. Indeed, a wave in the sea is not simply the continuation of the former wave; the whole ocean arises in each new wave. There is some influence of the previous wave, yes; but you also have to account for this additional dimension of time, which even Einstein did not see.

We are working with two dimensions of time: one is what we call the arrow of time, moving from the past to the future; and the other dimension is moving from transiency to transcendence. The instant of time is the moment when those two dimensions of time intersect one another.

If you consider your life as the object of your meditation, instead of choosing artificial objects upon which to meditate, then you will reach a great degree of realization. Concentrating on a divine name is going to highlight a certain quality that you want to develop. But looking at your life with an overview is going to reveal to you aspects, not just of your life, but aspects of the fundamental laws of the universe. That will awaken you. That is what awakening is: becoming a highly realized being; understanding your role in the universe and how it all functions; understanding the laws that you set into motion by your actions and even by your thoughts.

This is a very advanced form of meditation: you watch your life curve, as it is called. That is something you do more as you get older. You are able to look at your whole life as a film. If you are right in the midst of it, you cannot see what you might call the big picture. It requires you to have some distance from the situation—to look at things with an overview, as though you were flying a helicopter over the city.

You attempt to distinguish two things from this vantage point. First, you distinguish the sequence of events in your life. Perhaps you will not always see how one situation was the cause of the other; sometimes you will; what you sow you reap, and so on. But sometimes you do not see that connection. If you do not see that connection, then you ascribe it to fate. You think: "This was an accident," or "I cannot at all see why this happened."

The second thing that you want to distinguish in the big picture is the way that your personality has changed since you were a baby. You remember how you felt when you were seven years old, and when you were ten years old, and then fourteen, eighteen, and right into the present.

Then you combine these two. You connect the events with the way you felt. This is an opportunity to come to realizations that are going to produce great wisdom, and lead you toward awakening.

It is easier to see the impact of the events upon the way that your personality unfolded in the course of time. That is reasonably easy to see: how a traumatic event made you more cautious, or somehow has influenced your personality, has left its mark on your personality.

It is much more difficult to see the way in which your personality has influenced the events. That is what we want to see. You will find it formulated in the following words: "If I had been then what I am now, it would not have happened." Now you see the connection; that is, you see the influence of your personality upon the events. Remember Jung's words: if you do not face your shadow, it will come to you in the form of your fate.

This gives you a kind of grandstand view over your life. It seems that your life is moving like the diagram, or vector, of time, moving from left to right. This is enhanced if you are breathing in through your left nostril.

When you hold your breath, you are in a condition that is favorable to capturing the instant of time. When you exhale through the right nostril you are creating conditions that are favorable to forestalling the future. Forestalling—that is, having a kind of preview, entertaining some kind of projection as to how the future could be, or might be. We all have our plans, our projects, for the future—sometimes fraught with trepidation in a rather precarious world that could collapse at any moment.

So here we are, suspended between the past and the future in the instant of time. The thing about the instant of time is that it operates as a total break from the past and from your projections for the future. If you are in the moment of time then you can see the over-lap between the past and the future of your life. But if you think in terms of what the dervishes mean by the instant of time, then you are able to cut through, to make a clean break. It is like opening a new chapter in your life; you end one chapter, and open another. That which marks the transit from one chapter to the next is a pledge, a promise that you make to yourself.

Beware of getting bogged-in by your sense of guilt. The older you get, the more you confront your conscience; and, consequently, you are aware of all the mistakes that you have made. It is better to use the word *mistakes*. *Sin* is, of course, a dreadful word, as in "We are all miserable sinners." No, it is better to think: "Well, I have made a lot of mistakes." We are human, but it is difficult to forgive ourselves; we have this whole problem with guilt.

Still, what you have to do, if you want to open a new chapter, is to make a pledge not to continue doing the things you did before. All of a sudden you will find that you are a new person. You can hardly believe it; that pledge makes all the difference. You do not have to schlep your old personality with you throughout your life. You can be a new person from one second to the next.

Hujwiri, one of the wonderful Sufis who settled in India long before Khwaja Mu'in ad-Din Chishti, says, quoting the dervishes of his time: the instant of time is a sharp sword which cuts the guilt of the past and the concupiscence of the future.[2] We would say, rather, that it does offer some relief from the weight of our guilt, although we cannot ever be taken completely off the hook. We do bear some responsibility for the results

2 Hujwiri, *Kashf al-Mahjub*, 369.

of our actions. Still, there is a sense of atonement by dint of the pledge to do better, to be a better person.

But Hujwiri's comment has deeper implications: it speaks about freedom from conditioning. This is a much wider issue: to discover that you are free. There is a saying of Farid ad-Din 'Attar, "O man, if only you knew that you are free. It is your ignorance of your freedom that is your captivity."

You discover your freedom in the instant of time. In fact, you discover your freedom by pledging yourself! By pledging yourself you limit your freedom, but you are free to limit your freedom and, in so doing, you discover your freedom!

This was the ultimate objective of Buddha. After the forty-nine days he was under the bodhi tree, he said, "I have found the key to liberation!" It is the ending of conditioning. We generally do not realize the extent to which we are conditioned. We get into habits and we do not know how to free ourselves from those habits. We just continue doing things we have learned to do, taking life for granted.

Finding that you do not have to conform to what you have always done is discovering your freedom. This view of freedom was actuated in that extraordinary moment at the end of the training of the man Herrigel, when he was learning the art of archery.[3] On that last day, he asked his teacher to demonstrate. His teacher was blindfolded; it was in the dark; the target was very far away—and he hit the bull's-eye with the first go. Herrigel asked, "How on earth did you do it?" His teacher replied that: "The arrow guided my hand toward the target. The arrow was there before my hand

3 Eugene Herrigel, *Zen in the Art of Archery*, 58–59.

could loose it." What he is saying is that the causal link between the thrust of the hand and the arrow had come to a point of nil. There was no causality in it; he had overcome causality.

If you are aware of the modern theories, the non-deterministic theories, in physics, then you know that physics is looking into just that: the nondetermined. So far it has been exploring the determined. Creativity is the nondetermined. That is how you are able to find your freedom: by freeing yourself so that, for example, you do not compose like your predecessors composed. You have to find a new way.

So, imagine that you are going through life, being a new being, finding your own way of being totally free from the past. You do have to learn it first. You know the past, but, as Stravinsky said in our classes on music, "Learn the music of the past and then forget it."

After holding your breath, you exhale through the right nostril. Now you are creating conditions that are favorable toward forestalling the future. We are always projecting the future. Especially when you are on a retreat, you make plans more than ever before; you cannot do things, so you keep making plans.

This is where the Sufi practice called *muhasaba* comes in. That is, you confront your motivations with the power of truth. You ask yourself: "Why do I want to do this? To what extent am I motivated by hoping to get something out of it, and to what extent am I motivated by my dedication to a cause?" We are not saying that you are a bad person if you are trying to get something out of it. We are saying that you must be very clear as to what you hope to gain out of it. There is a balance here between personal needs or desires, and dedication to the ideal; and the balance point is different for each person.

If you are following the path of spirituality, then you measure exactly what you need in terms of personal necessities, but you are essentially dedicated to your ideal. If not, then spirituality, or what people call spirituality, is the most utter selfishness. To hope to attain illumination for yourself is selfishness. That is why Buddha himself says it is only to be able to illuminate other people, but not for yourself. That is why the Sufis say renounce the world, renounce yourself, and then renounce renunciation—out of love. Examine your plans for the future in the light of all of this, seeing very clearly what your motivations are.

Then, as you breathe in through the right nostril, you see how, indeed, your plans, your prefiguration of the future, exercise a pull on you out of the past. If you did not have those plans for the future, you would be bogged down in the past. You frequently find cases of this among older people. They are still living in the past, bogged-in to their memories of the past. They are not making plans for the future.

There is a formula which will help you remember this: "The pull of the future is stronger than the push of the past."[4] It represents a whole new approach in science: the nondeterministic theories of modern physics. An article in a scientific journal some years ago showed that the evolution of the chemistry on Planet Earth which led toward the formation of the human being would not have been thinkable if the advent of

---

4 This phrase is attributed to Leonhard Euler (1707–83), a Swiss mathematician whose prolific works treat all major branches of mathematics.

the human being had not already been foreseen. Teilhard de Chardin says that "You did not know what those several threads were converging toward until you discovered that they were converging toward making you.[5] You were already thought of before the beginning of the universe. This recalls the words of Christ: "You loved me before the beginning of the universe."[6] It was out of love that God created the universe, rather than out of a wish to know God's own Self.

So, that is a very important formula—you must always have that in mind: the pull of the future. We have been brought up to think in terms of causality; for instance, what you sow you reap, or, the past influences the future. It does. But there is also the pull of the future that is not yet here. It is on its way. Be purpose oriented instead of causally causated. Think in terms of the purpose of life, rather than dwelling too much on causality.

When you hold your breath after being pulled by the future, by your plans for the future, you realize that your plans could break down. Not only that, but you realize that you are limiting the possibilities of the future by your planning. Just as you have limited yourself by the conditioning of the past, you are also limiting yourself by your forestalling of the future.

Life requires of you an acceptance that things could turn out to be better, or less good, than you had hoped. "You cannot play dice with God," as Einstein says, "or God does not play dice with you."[7] There is an element

5 Pierre Teilhard de Chardin (1881–1955) was a French scientist and Catholic theologian, whose main work was reconciling Christianity with the social and mental evolution of humanity. See *The Phenomenon of Man* for a presentation of his thought.
6 John 17:24.
7 See Frithjof Capra, *The Tao of Physics*, 311.

of unknowing, of the unpredictable, the improvisable. It is a very extraordinary feeling: to be free from your plans for the future. It is somewhat like a blank slate. When you have found freedom from the future, you gain an even greater degree of freedom from the past than you realized when you made that pledge.

However, when you hold your breath after inhaling through both nostrils you discover a totally different condition of time. It is not the instant of time. It is what we understand by eternity. If you look at the pendulum again, there are three important points in the motion of the pendulum: left, and right, and then the point at which the pendulum is suspended on your hand or on a nail. That third point represents what we ascribe to fate.

Here we have the confrontation between our free will and, let us say, our programming. You cannot simply say that we are programmed; if we were merely programmed, we would be like puppets in the hand of some wizard. Once again, it would be that exaggerated sense of otherness: God up there. It is much more subtle than that. You could say that the programming of the universe evolves in the course of time. You could even say that our incentive exercises an influence on the programming of the universe—not just the programming of our own lives, but the programming of the universe.

If Sheldrake's theories are demonstrated, that is, confirmed by research, we would have definite evidence that there is feedback from the existential level into the programming of the universe. That would mean, putting it in very simplistic language, that God has to take into account our decisions. The question is whether

God proposes and man disposes, or whether it is man proposes and God disposes.

You get to a point in your meditation when your need for realization requires you to have some sense of the meaningfulness in the programming of the universe. So then you are doing exactly what physicists are doing today. Physicists are doing it with a lot of skills that have developed during the training of the mind of the physicists. The contemplative is doing it using different skills. But, ultimately, both are seeking illumination. In fact, illumination is really what we mean by awakening.

You understand that you cannot work this out, you cannot achieve this objective, with your ordinary, commonplace mind. You have already learned, in the first steps of this retreat, to modulate your thinking into the internal state, into what we call the implicate state. Then you learned to modulate your thinking into the transcendental dimension.

The paradox about all of this is that the programming of the universe can never be the object of our understanding, because we embody that programming. Or let us say that the thinking of God can never be the object of our thinking, because we think the way God thinks, except that the thinking of God has become funneled down, and even distorted, in each fragment of itself.

If you fragment a hologram, each fragment will act like the hologram but a little less well. The more you fragment it, the less well it functions in comparison with the whole hologram. In infinite regress, you could reach a point when it begins to function as a fragment and not as the whole hologram—a point at which it has lost the sense of the whole. That is what we are doing, unless we discover the whole hologram working as our thinking. Newton said, "I think like God thinks."[8] He realized that the universe is thinking as our thinking, and that we limit it. We are like the fragment of the hologram that has lost the sense of the whole.

What we mean by awakening is a state in which the whole, the thinking of the whole universe, flashes into our consciousness without limitation. That is what is called a state of samadhi. It does not mean that we are grasping the programming: we are grasping the intention.

The programming is customized by the intention. Hazrat Inayat Khan says that awakening is discovering the divine intention,[9] and, we would add, opening up our intention so that it coincides with the divine intention. That is why Christ said, "Thy will be done."[10] That is why, in this meditation, you have been attempting to discover your intention. When you look at the past, you see that your mistakes could be attributed to your intention at the time. And when you look into the future, you are beginning to scan your intention; you are beginning to ascertain what your intention is.

Ultimately, you lift your consciousness to the point from which, wherever you look, you see the intention; whereas, in your normal understanding, things seem to happen by accident, or there is so much incongruity in

---

8 Isaac Newton (1642–1726) was an English mathematician and physicist whose major impact was the discovery of the laws of motion, gravitation, and calculus. In his later years his interest turned to theology and alchemy.
9 *TThe Alchemy of Happiness*, 182.
10 Matthew 6:10.

the way things happen that it is difficult to accept that there could be meaningfulness behind it all.

We realize that we are raising important metaphysical questions. In the higher levels of meditation, that is precisely what you meet: metaphysical questions. Like, Is everything programmed? or What is the role of free will? More paradoxically: Is there such a thing as randomness; that is, accident? Or is randomness a transitional stage; that is, the way that an orderliness breaks down so that it can be replaced by a new orderliness?

It would be very frightening to be delivered into the hands of a random universe that could run amok at any time. In fact, that is the very crux of our fears, the kind of fear that people had in a concentration camp; that not just the human mind, but the human heart, has gone amok, has gone mad. It is unbelievable. Perhaps we are not even afraid of death: what we are afraid of is that it is a catastrophe, that the order of the universe has gone wrong. If we could be convinced that there is meaningfulness in our death, it would be much more acceptable—in fact, it would be welcome.

If you have done astral travel, then you know that you can see without eyes, and you can hear without ears, and you can move about without legs and wings. Once you have had that experience it confirms what Murshid says: "You can raise your consciousness above your earthly condition."[11]

You have a sense of having awakened from unreality, as, when the whole scene of unreality away, then reality strikes you with great power.[12] That is why the Tibetans are using

---

11 *The Alchemy of Happiness*, 9.
12 Inayat Khan, *The Complete Sayings*, 163.

meditation as a preparation for death: so that you know what to expect; you have already trained yourself.

The secret offered by the Tibetans is to teach yourself to awaken in the dream state. Then teach yourself to awaken in sleep without dreams. Then you imagine how it would be to awaken past the threshold of death. You are already forestalling your resurrection, which is what we were doing with our *ajsam* body. Working with the subtle body is the first step. It is called fashioning the body of resurrection. There you have a definite impact. Your free will is exercising itself in deciding the way in which you want to shape your subtle body.

It is very difficult to shape your physical body; we have the body the way it is. But your subtle body can more readily be shaped the way you want it to be. We have to be very clear about that, because you will find it is rather like the voice of Caruso. You will find the celestial core present within its distortion. You will find that the way that the subtle body is formed does evidence the defilement in your emotions and in your thinking. It is the picture of Dorian Gray.[13] It is a wonderful feedback system: you can see right away where the distortions are. The beauty is that you can always compare the distortion with the original model.

Imagine that you had a hologram. Perhaps you have seen the hologram where you can focus your perspective in such a way that you see the Shroud of Turin, the image of Christ on the Shroud of Turin; and then, if you shift your perspective, you see a painting of Christ's

---

12 The 1891 novel by Oscar Wilde, *The Picture of Dorian Gray*, supposes that Dorian remains youthful and attractive, while an artist's portrait of him ages and grows grotesque with his profligate lifestyle.

face. You can toggle between the two very easily, surprisingly. Of course, those pictures do not mesh totally; it is very difficult to superimpose them. You can do the same thing trying to have a sense of the shape of your etheric body. We are working with the aura because it is easier.

Think that you are a being of light, you are like a statue made of the fabric of light. You can see that it definitely has a shape, which is rather similar to the physical body, and especially the face. Within it there seems to be a core, which is sublimely beautiful—so beautiful that you cannot believe that it is you. This is illustrated by the voice of Caruso, within its distortion. It is in its distortion—within it.

You could highlight one or the other: your pristine, celestial condition or the defilement and distortion that has occurred in the process of becoming. Then you match the two, and you see how they differ. In order to recover the voice of Caruso they had to get a gramophone of the old days, the kind of machine with which they recorded the voice of Caruso in the first place, and compare the frequencies with modern technology. Then they knew how to reverse the distortions. So, it is possible: you can reverse your distortions to get back to the pristine state.

But our objective is not to return to the place where we were before we were involved in the process of becoming. This had been the theory of one of the early Sufis, al-Junayd; he was a contemporary of al-Hallaj, who did not agree.[14] As Pir-o-Murshid articulated, at

14 Al-Junayd (d. 910) is a major exponent of sobriety in Sufism, as distinguished from the ecstatic approach of al-Hallaj. See *The Life, Personality and Writings of al Junayd* by Ali Hassan Abdel Kader.

the *malakut* level, the celestial level, you have two types of souls: those whom we call angels, who have not yet incarnated and who are rather childlike, but very beautiful; and then the mature souls who have resurrected and who have reached that level, the *malakut* level, on the return journey, so to speak, from incarnation.[15] These latter souls are a combination of a child and an elder at the same time. It is a strange kind of reconciliation of the irreconcilables.

Once you have worked with meshing the way that your aura looks with the core of the aura, you can start forestalling how you would like to be. You have already worked with trying to imagine how you would like to be as a personality. Now you are working with meshing the way that your etheric body, or your aura, looks, with the way you would like it to look—but as a picture, as a form.

We could give an example of this in music: we did this at the music school in Paris with Nadia Boulanger, and she said, "All right now, you have composed this. Now imagine how it could be."[16] You see that your composition could be better. If you are satisfied with your composition, then of course there is no way of progressing.

We have the power of projecting how we could be. And even that is limited by where we are in our life. The painting of an artist, or the composition of a composer, reflects their degree of evolution. A composer cannot compose a piece of music that is more advanced

---

15 *The Inner Life*, 162.
16 Nadia Boulanger (1887–1979) was a French musician, composer, and conductor, who taught students, including Pir Vilayat, at the École Normale de Musique in Paris.

than the composer is in the composer's own being; or a painter, the same thing applies to a painter.

But somehow we have within ourselves the propensity to represent something beyond our reach, or what we think is beyond our reach. It is what Poincaré said: you can always imagine a number larger than the largest number you have imagined so far. In the same way, you can always imagine a larger, more wonderful perfection than the one you have imagined so far. This is embodied in our representation of God. We limit our representation of God by, let us say, the stature of our being. But we have the propensity of imagining God to be even more wonderful than we have imagined God so far. And by doing this we are extending the horizons of our own being.

This is the role of creativity. You could apply it to everyday life. In fact, you should apply it to everyday life if you really want to follow the spiritual path. That is, you catch yourself being disgruntled, and you think to yourself: "Why am I disgruntled, I should be dancing with joy!" You can really stop yourself from being disgruntled. You have a frown on your face, and you remind yourself: "I should have light in my eyes! What am I doing? I am spending my time having this ugly frown on my face, and it is not doing any good to anybody, nor to myself, I am bogged down in my own trip." That is where your morning meditations should help you. Apply them in everyday life—but you have to remind yourself.

There is a piece of music that has been very meaningful to me: the Madrigals of Monteverdi conducted by Nadia Boulanger. It describes, on the one hand, the monks, who are in a very high state of attunement;

and then the people coming to the church, who are expressing a longing for the monks to inspire them. The monks are there in their attunement, and the people are down there, trying to get inspired. Then you have the fanfare in the street, the drunken people, and you think, "How could Monteverdi do that to us?" But, actually, he is describing the jester.

The monks were not quite able to convey the message to the people. The jester can plug into the mentality of the people much better, and if a good jester, then is able to convey wisdom by using very simple methods of expression; in fact, by using humor. So the jester is like a master who is subjecting himself or herself to the derision of people in service of conveying wisdom.

Maybe it is better to be a jester than a monk. A monk tends to be sanctimonious, and that is a danger of spirituality. Being sanctimonious—that is, taking yourself seriously, considering yourself to be a master, better than other people—that terrible mentality that you find mostly in spiritual groups. Our path is the freedom from the guru. You burn the idol. In fact, it is a line of Jalal ad-Din Rumi's: the pir is the destroyer of the idol that people would like to make of him.

Chapter 13

Being in the World

When you have shared bread at the same table, there is a bond that has been established. There is also a sense of commitment, which you would like to share with others. You may feel like the custodian of a message, or that you are carrying something sacred in your being, just like the people who have received the host in Communion.

That is what makes the initiate: someone who is connected in some way by a spiritual pledge, by a kind of inner commitment, to an ideal. As Pir-o-Murshid says, if you have commitment, then you need to bring yourself in trim, you need to train yourself, you need to prepare yourself to attune yourself.[1] Doing this in our daily meditations is wonderful, but the stress of our lives is such that we cannot afford as much time as we would like in order to do that. We need to see how we can pursue this training, not just in our meditation, but also throughout our everyday life.

It requires a continual reminder. Remember these words of Hazrat Inayat Khan: you get to a point when you are able to raise your consciousness at any moment

---

1 *The Path of Initiation*, 72.

from your earthly condition.[2] That would include being in the middle of a real-life situation, even amongst people who have no idea what it means. At those moments you see yourself in the universe, and you see how your consciousness can be focused one way or the other. It could be focused on your earthly condition, as when you think of yourself as an individual amongst other individuals, with a job and family, seeking some kind of entertainment, or gratification. Or then, you think, "Yes, it is true that I need to contribute to our society. I have a role to play. I have a responsibility. In order to fulfill that responsibility better, I must not let myself be bogged-in to the commonplace kind of emotions that I find amongst people." This applies particularly to the very demeaning emotions with which you are confronted, and by which you are affected, just by watching TV.

The very grossness that is coming through our society is a matter for concern; but without being judgmental, you simply need to feel that you are seeking for your ideal.

Somehow you have been able to catch a glimpse of it. It is not just utopic. There are moments when you are actually experiencing it; it is not just a projection of the mind. There have been moments when your whole being was imbued with it very deeply, and transformed by it, transfigured. That is the experience of God, rather than the concept of God.

The sense of being entrusted with something very sacred is also based upon real experience. You cannot define it exactly. But, having felt the sacredness of the immaculate state at the core of your being, you realize that you need to honor it and to protect it. Doing so

2 *The Vision of God and Man*, 91.

helps you to fulfill your purpose in life. You actually begin to see the purpose. You can see meaningfulness. There is no need for blind faith.

We have learned to turn within while still being in touch with the environment. Do not let yourself be pulled into the environment emotionally, to be pulled down to the lowest common denominator. In your understanding, do not allow yourself to be caught in the way other people think—then you would lose the freedom of your own thinking.

When speaking to a person you might feel you can see how that person is thinking. You can see that, of course, they are thinking the way they are thinking, and they are convinced of it—each person according to his or her vantage point. Also, people are behaving according to their understanding. You get to a point when you can see all of that. You are not judgmental, you are not judging. It is like it is with children: there are different levels of classes the children go to. You involve yourself without losing your inner freedom. You maintain your inner freedom. But somehow you play ball, like you play ball with children. It does not mean that you think as a child does, but that you can enjoy the way the child thinks.

You are protected by the emotion that we call *vairagya*, which has generally been translated as "indifference." Do not think of it as indifference; think of it as unconditional love. It has no personal implications. It is all absolutely beautiful. There is caring, and there is sharing; there is freedom in it, and there is involvement. But it is an involvement which does not limit your real freedom. It only limits your circumstantial freedom.

Life is a wonderful opportunity in which to practice meditation. Every now and again you can, for example, close your eyes and see how things look as seen from inside. There is a practice you could use. Imagine that your two eyes are the headlamps of a car. With closed eyelids, you project them forward as you exhale. Turn your eyeballs upward as you inhale. Then hold your breath and think of yourself as being pure intelligence, rather than consciousness. Consciousness is receptive, whereas intelligence is active. As you exhale, you cast your glance forward.

If you keep doing this exercise, you will eventually be able to open your eyes and keep your glance focused as though it were two beams of light. Normally, if you open your eyes, they would be forced into focus by the environment. Do not allow this to happen. Keep peering through the physical world, just like an x-ray passing through a wall.

To be able to do this practice effectively, you want to develop a lot of light in your eyes. You can do this in your morning meditations, and anytime during the day. Just think of having a lot of light in your eyes. That in itself will have an effect upon your attunement. You become much happier when you have light in your eyes.

There is a sense of bearing responsibility for your life and, therefore, having to exercise some kind of control over situations. It can extend to wanting to control other people. It is, for example, rather natural that we feel a responsibility to control our children. However, the secret of what we call sovereignty is to enlist people's ideals—if they are in resonance with your own ideals—by showing them how they can fulfill their ideals. You are not subjecting other people to your vision of things; you are helping people who cannot, by themselves, fulfill their vision to achieve their vision. Maybe you have more insight and more mastery than some people do, and, consequently, instead of being despotic you are helping people to fulfill their ideals.

You realize that the way things look is deceptive. We have already said that to develop your intuition, you have to turn inside. At every moment you have to be able to look inside, and to reach the other person from inside. What you discover is the commonality between you and that person. There is a sense of understanding one another which you would not have if you had not allowed your consciousness to reach right into the consciousness of that person.

If you get into the consciousness of a typical person, you see just how limited their grasp of meaningfulness is. If your objective is awakening, you need to protect your realization against points of view that weaken it or destroy it. When you are continually trying to see how you can harmonize with the arguments of other people that go counter to your realization, you see how easily you could be drawn into thinking as other people do. That is where you need to have some kind of buffer, some kind of protection. You need to find your own space in the middle of your commitment in life, your involvement with people in life—still have your own space. That is the clue to protecting your realization.

Do not simply concur with people, or imitate the way that everybody thinks as they talk. But do realize that is what is happening to people. The guideline here is that you are continually conscious of your ideal. Always go back to fundamentals. Give yourself some space, and ask yourself: "What am I really seeking in life?" In order to understand this completely you have to be conscious of the divine perfection coming through your being. This perfection is being limited by the conditions, and it is constantly trying to break through those worldly conditions.

That is the way to find inner freedom. There is a kind of entropy in human emotions. Emotions tend to sink down into the common denominator, so that you continually need to seek inspiration. Getting into the consciousness of a master or discovering the angelic spheres are the ways in which we let ourselves be inspired, or uplifted. As a consequence, we are able to avoid slipping into that common denominator, that kind of entropy that takes place at the level of thought as well as the level of emotion.

At a certain moment detachment, which is the buffer, becomes so very important that you do definitely cut out the impressions of the outside world for a time, for a short time. You find that these impressions are deceptive. Also, you sense that there is a meaningfulness behind what appears at the surface that you do not see as long as you are caught up in the usual way of thinking. You have to protect yourself from this commonplace mode of thinking because it is extremely persistent. It is addictive.

Through your detachment you realize the relationship between your emotional attunement and your understanding. It is only by allowing your emotions to be highly attuned that you will be able to see things differently.

As Pir-o-Murshid indicates, you become aware of the way identifying with your physical condition entraps you in a very limited purview. Raise yourself from this earthly condition, considering it as a scaffolding, as an underpinning. This is where God-consciousness will make all the difference. If you are trying to reach upward, you are limiting yourself; you are limiting your ascent by the notion of yourself as the one who is wishing it. It is much more effective to think the other way around: "The divine perfection is trying to come through my imperfection. There is a divine fulfillment taking place as long as I do not obstruct it or limit it by my personal way of looking at things."

Always be on the lookout for what is enacted behind the situations. Let us take a very concrete example. You are in a situation in which you need to make a decision; you have to choose between two options. You are dithering all the time because both have their pros and their cons. You consider one, but then you think of its disadvantages; then you think of the other one, and that has its disadvantages, too.

It just depends upon your attunement. If you are in a very high attunement you decide on option one. You are aware of what sacrifices it entails, but still, it is so important to you that the sacrifices do not seem very important. Then, if you slip down into a lower level of attunement, you think: "It is true, these are things I was prepared to sacrifice; but it is a pity, because I do like them." There you are, right back to the common denominator again. So you can see that your attunement has a decisive impact upon your decisions in life, your options in life, your choices. Now, there are some guidelines which will be useful in situations such as this.

Your familiarity with the divine names will help you to see more clearly what we mean by the issues that are enacted behind your problems. For example, if I choose option A, I will develop power; but it will be at the cost of something that I would like to do. So that is the issue. Is that important enough for me to be prepared to make that sacrifice? If you choose option B, then you will not develop power, but it is possible that you will develop other qualities.

For example, it might be a very difficult situation in which your decision causes pain to another person. If you choose option B, you are not causing pain but you are sacrificing the power that you would have gained if you had chosen option A. There you have a typical case. You have to make a choice, not between two actions, but between two values. What do I value more?

There is a further factor; that is, if you choose option A, what are the qualities that will be unleashed in the person who is involved in the problem? If you choose option B, what would be the qualities that person will develop or would lose? For example, when you choose option A it means that you are hard on a person. But on the other hand, the consequence may be that the person gains strength, instead of that person being beholden to your compassion. There you see that it is the qualities that are the issues, and that dictate your action.

These are the guidelines: you are always on the lookout for the qualities, and the names are the language, of those qualities. More importantly, you find that the assessment that you make about the qualities is relative. We tend to get caught very easily in the illusion, the unreality. There comes a point where you feel that you are involved in a game in which you do not see clearly; you are caught in an illusion. That is the moment when you feel as though the world is stifling, and you need to break out of that unreality. All that you have been do-ing proves to be only palliative. You are not grappling with the real issue.

The real issue is, of course, the very purpose of God: that each being should become a beautiful person. Let us say this from another point of view: the issue is that through this whole struggle of life we each become a beautiful person, because it is God becoming a beauti-ful person as us. It is not just our personal well-being, or our personal purpose, that is at stake. This makes it easier to give up things that you would have liked to do. It also makes you feel happier about taking respon-sibility for people. By becoming a beautiful person you will help the people around you to become beautiful.

So, now we have a few tools at our disposal as we turn within. We can see the picture of Dorian Gray our-selves, much better than in our ordinary consciousness. We can feel that very fine barometer which Pir-o-Murshid calls the spirit: whether the spirit is humiliated, or whether the spirit is uplifted.

Another source of feedback is the way that people react to you. It is a feedback. You can see how people detect your ego, and they counter it with their ego. Sometimes you feel disapproval. If you feel disapproval, or if you feel criticism, listen to it. There is generally some ground for it. Maybe they are mis-assessing you, misunderstanding you—of course you have to account for that. Still, there is always something there that you need to pick up and learn from.

We have also discovered some clues from our medita-tions that will be useful in person-to-person commu-nication. From the moment that you realize the value of silence, you realize how your thinking gets bogged down in the explicatory mode, the mode in which you explain. So, while communicating with a person, be aware that your deeper meaning needs to bypass the words. As it is said, the meaning is between the words. It gets communicated without the words, and it is by your emotional attunement that it is communicated. Your emotional attunement is something that people pick up right away.

When you are speaking, you realize just how inadequate your words are, but it is a means of communicating. Most conversations are not particularly brilliant; they are just a means of communicating. At times it is better to open up and say things that are nonsense, rather than not speaking. Imagine you are in an elevator and somebody comes in. There is a cold silence, and you think, "Oh, I should say something." So you say, "What a nice day!"but you forgot that it is raining. It is okay; it does not matter. You are just communicating.

An advanced way of communicating, which you could call the way of the initiate, is to meditate while you are talking with someone. For example, you could identify with your aura and be conscious of the light around you and the light in your cells, while you are talking. It does not have to be an important conversation; it could be about anything. That person picks it up, and all of a sudden you see that their eyes begin to glitter with light. You have not said anything, but they feel it. There is an inner communication between people; a tacit communication takes place that bypasses the verbal conversation.

If you apply the technique of considering your glance as active, instead of thinking that your eyes are the passive receptacles of experience, you will begin to see what we call the eternal face behind the physical face of the person. It is so beautiful that you are yourself uplifted by it.

You do not have to look for beautiful music, or beautiful churches or paintings. You can find beauty in a face that for all intents and purposes does not appear particularly beautiful. Behind the mask you can see beauty. Jalal ad-Din Rumi said, "If only you could see your face through my eyes, you would realize how beautiful you are." People can see themselves through your eyes. You can help them in one of the most important aspects of the personality: their self-esteem. It also confirms your utopic thoughts that, in fact, there is beauty behind whatever appears at the surface in the universe.

So you are continually guarding your emotional attunement from slipping into a low-key condition. At the same time, you are outraged by any offense against honesty, and outraged against rank selfishness. In a way, you are exalting in joy and, at the same time, enduring terrible suffering. Your heart is broken, there is so much suffering in the world.

You are so full of joy; yet, as you become aware of the suffering of people around you, it is very difficult to maintain that level of jubilation which you encountered when you lifted your consciousness upward. You find that you are being tested in life: are you able to be full of joy and, at the same time, have a broken heart?

You may also find that you feel precarious and strong at the same time. As Pir-o-Murshid says, be able to reconcile the perfection of your divine inheritance with the imperfection of your idiosyncrasies.[3] He calls it the

3 *Philosophy, Psychology, Mysticism*, 220.

aristocracy of the soul, together with the democracy of the ego both together, not one or the other. If you tilt too much in the direction of your personal dimension, you have a sense of inadequacy; you have a bad self-image. If you tilt too much in the direction of your divine inheritance, you could become sanctimonious; you might think of yourself as superior to others. It is very difficult to reconcile these two.

Again, the thought of the voice of Caruso is very helpful—even more so if you can really see in your being the beauty and the defilement at the same time. See them both. The way of reconciling them is to know that you can actually reverse the defilement.

We would probably all like some wise person to tell us what our purpose is in life. There are several ways of looking at it. Some people would like to have a clue as to their vocation, especially younger people. Or people can get to a crossroads in their life; for example, their father wanted them to be a lawyer and, at a certain moment, they regret that they did not become a musician. So you ask yourself: "Should I give up my lawyer's job and start playing the piano? It does not make sense in terms of the economy. And in terms of my being. . . ."

You see how easily you can get to a point when you would like to go to a guru and ask, "What should I do?" Or then, in personal relationships, "Should I marry this person or that one? With these kind of questions, you would like to have some guidance. "What is my purpose in life? What am I doing?"

Murshid is saying that the purpose of life is like the horizon. You think, "This is my purpose," and then you realize that there is another purpose behind it. It is multidimensional also. It is not just in terms of an advance in time; there are levels of purposefulness.

For example, "Yes, I want to become a cellist." Okay. Why do you want to become a cellist? "Well, I do not know, I just want to become a cellist." Then, there is a higher purpose behind it: "Because I find exaltation in music." Okay, that is a higher purpose. There might be a still higher purpose. "It is because music gives me a sense of understanding life that I cannot find in other things." That would be a still higher purpose. There would be other purposes; for example, "I like to convey the joy that I experience in music to other people. The reason I want to be a cellist is not to play to myself but to play to other people." There is always another purpose.

The most important way of looking at it is that you create your purpose as you advance, instead of thinking it is already there. You say you would like to know your purpose; you create your purpose—that is how you discover it.

It is very paradoxical in science, for example, that an electron just finds another orbital. The orbital does not exist; somehow the electron creates it as it reaches a high level of energy. It is not like the rails of a locomotive; it is more like the pathways of the airplanes in the sky. They make their own pathway: it does not already exist for them, pre-prepared.

There is a saying of Kabir: life is a field, all you have to do is to cultivate it. If you want to know your purpose, you do not have to look very far. Everywhere around you there are problems. The question is, "How can I best provide a service?" Murshid says something very paradoxical here. He says by pursuing a purpose

one develops power, and with that power one can opt
for a more challenging purpose.[4] Then you gain a further power, which again will want to face a still greater
challenge.

But the paradoxical thing is that your purpose limits
your power. That is, what you try to get out of it limits
your power. Your personal power has its limits. You see
this when you have an object in view and you want to
accomplish it. You are developing power in order to
accomplish that object, but that object is going to determine the kind of power that you are able to develop.

If your purpose is service, your power is infinite. That
is a very strange ingredient in our being which, in the
tradition of the Sufis, they call magic, magical power. It
is a kind of inner attunement that makes things happen.
You still have to do something, but that attunement
has a magical power. The key to it is to be aware of the
divine power in your being.

Divine power is something that you come across
particularly in deep meditation. You cannot believe
the power that is coming through, and you know you
could never ascribe it to your own power, your own ego
power. It is like cosmic emotion coming through, like
the emotion that moves the universe and the planets.
This was expressed poetically when Jalal ad-Din Rumi
said, "I could flood the world with my tears; or, I could
burn the world with my flame." It is a sense of something very intense, present in the depth of your being;
but you do not ascribe it to yourself—it does not feel
like your personal power. You can use words for it for
example, *ishq Allah maʿbud Allah*, signifying the divine

---

4 *The Alchemy of Happiness*, 177.

nostalgia. But these are just words, and the experience itself is beyond any words you could use.

Perhaps you enjoy thunder and lightning in a storm. Pablo Casals used to live, before the Spanish revolution, in a little chalet by the sea in San Salvador. He used to play the cello there. People there were bathing in the sun, although you never saw him on the beach at those times. But when there was a storm there were no bathers, but Pablo Casals, sure enough, would be walking on the beach with his celebrated frown on his face, braving the thunder and the lightning. These natural forces can symbolize our outrage.

Your quest for the angelic level needs to be reconciled with the kind of maturity that comes to a being who stands for righteousness against dishonesty or exploitation—in fact, all of the terrible things that we are witnessing today in our world. That is the emotion of outrage. Thunder and lightning seem to resonate with that sense of outrage in your being; they highlight it, awaken it.

So maybe we have to learn how to reconcile the rainbow and the lightning. We have seen this, once, in the mountains: a rainbow and lightning at the same time. The objective is not to return to the state in which we were in the angelic spheres before incarnating. Our purpose is to become fully realized, mature angels, like Saint Michael.

It is good to have these clichés, as you might call them, in our minds, these pictures of that to which we aspire. That is the role of myth. Never think, "Oh, he can do it but I cannot. Let Christ do it. Poor me." That is why Buddha said, "You must try for your own awakening, for your own liberation." Do not depend upon anybody to liberate you or to awaken you. Awakening does not happen by the grace of the guru.

Wild Carrot. Photograph ©Walter Chappell.

Baby Carrot. Photograph ©Walter Chappell.

Appendix

The Life and Work of Walter Chappell

Since 1974, the transcendental aspect of Walter Chapell's work has been expressed in a unique new direction: the use of electrophotography to reveal the fluorescent emanations of energy systems integral to living things. Technically, to do this he places plants or parts of them on the surface of a photographic plate. When this living organic matter is introduced into a high voltage field, its electrons are changed into photons and, for a sparkling instant, they produce an image of the plant's life force. Even though achieved in complete darkness without lens or camera, these are not surface images like an X-ray or photogram, for they spatially objectify the energy field within the plant's organic structure.

Although this procedure is similar to Kirlian photography, the creative basis for these resplendent black-and-white prints is closer to the studies of radionics by George and Marjorie De La Warr, which imply dynamic interrelations between human thought and a universal *élan vital*. Chappell refers to these images of life's radiance as his *Metaflora* series to suggest a documentary that is both objective and spiritual. For him, these ephemeral experiences captured on film are "equivalents" simultaneously merging his own energies with those of the plant to create an image densely saturated with information on many levels. These are conjunctions that provide the opportunity, in Chappell's words, "to create a new image of understanding for my senses, and to unify my discovery of nature with the growing discovery of my inner being."

Born in 1925 in Portland, Oregon, Walter Chappell studied architectural drawing at Benson Polytechnical School, and piano and musical composition at Ellison-White Conservatory of Music. From 1943 to 1946 he served in the United States 13th Airborne Division. Chappell's friendship with Minor White, which began in 1942, was renewed in San Francisco in 1947; and although Chappell's creative interests would turn to photography, his main pursuits then were music, painting, and writing. *Logue and Glyphs*, a book of his poetry, was published in 1948.

In 1957, Chappell settled in Rochester, New York, to study printmaking technique with Minor White. Here Chappell wrote and edited for *Aperture* magazine and assisted White in workshops. *Gestures of Infinity*, a collection of images and poetry was produced in 1957. In 1961, *Under the Sun*, images by Walter Chappell, Nathan Lyons, and Syl Labrot, was published by George Braziller.

After serving as curator at George Eastman House for three years, Chappell founded and directed a gallery/archive in New York during the years 1962–65. His growing interest in the imagery of the human form in nature and in experimental filmmaking led him, after a brief time in Big Sur, to Taos, New Mexico, where he photographed landscapes and nudes, and studied Native American ceremonial life.

Following a move to San Francisco, where he worked from 1970 to 1974, he began experimental work with electrophotography: high voltage–high frequency electron imagery of living plants. This work was presented in his *Metaflora Portfolio*, the 1980 publication of which was supported in part by a grant from the National Endowment for the Arts.

In 1987 Chappell moved to the remote village of El Rito, New Mexico, and from there he continued to exhibit, lecture, give workshops, and make field trips. His main concern was the preparation of a retrospective monograph of his work in photography entitled *Collected Light*.

In 1978 Chappell wrote,

> The ideas hovering over my four-year preoccupation with producing the *Metaflora Portfolio* stem deeply from early wonderment and experiences pondered with living with plants. Most of my childhood unfolded in the greenhouse and garden of my grandparents, who were florists in Oregon during the great depression, from 1925 till 1947. Growing up was an involvement imbosked in plant life: watering, planting, weeding, watching, gathering, and arranging floral displays, which was our livelihood. Funerals and weddings were the occasions for Grandmother Addie's masterworks in floral symphony.
>
> There was always the excitement of working and repose in the long days and nights of the growing season. Bulbs were dug up and cellared to rest for replanting in spring as the winter arrived. Some innate capacities emerged and developed in this background of foliage, being influenced by and, in turn, finding ways to influence plant growth by means of direct seeing-participation. The

care of plants and maintenance of some kind of garden has ever since found its place within the changing circumstances of my life."

Writing of his *Metaflora* project, he continued:

In this octave of photography, the plant-form has become the camera-opening upon a perspective where life-forms express light constantly, simultaneously enacting photography-photosynthesis.

Although I experience the medium of photography as a rapidly adjusting balance of both art and science, it is not my intention to explain, nor furnish with logic, either domain. My wish is to share these impressions which create for me deeper insights into and through the continuous surface our sense seem to weave as a shroud camouflaging intelligence, flattening one sphere to many circles.

Looking at and empathizing with these images seems to evoke a mental energy of mercurial sensuousness, which at once escapes the orbit of time-space words and concepts. These positive silver prints, realized on return from a threshold of visibility, are exposures made from a layer of organic life we may not see, though we may sometimes sense with the whole body.

In this camera obscura of open air, focused and autographed through attraction of positron and electron, only pulsating sound and a faint glow of ultraviolet signal the event of recondite sidereal luminescence. An immence presence of air-piercing ozone penetrates the sense of smell, prolonging peaks of mental excitement retained during the awesome transport between extra-sensory openings and closings. The plant organ usurps the camera-persona there, in dark intimacy with film, as avalanching electrons leap into light-forms, precisely exposing the energy emanations occurring spontaneously with the meeting of the three forces—positron, electron, and this moment of life—on negative film.

The realized print survives as an image of direct contact with the bioplasmic counterpart which pervades, and may contain, our physical world of appearances.

Attempting to imagine the electromagnetic spectrum as a whole (perhaps one hundred octaves) with the steps we, the living, traverse beyond our beholding powers, draws one nearer to the present footprint on infinity. Our sense perceptions at their best, and least transient, register visibility a few octaves below the middle range of a cosmic scale including all that is.

To choose one leaf, one blossom, plucking them from the countless organs of foliage sensualizing the skin of this planet continuously with living forces, allowing these organs by hand to manifest a presence, being all at once light in total darkness—this is somehow the way everything is always present. Perceiving more and longer without concept, as we may be always becoming what everything is, we live what we are in this spectrum, rarely knowing what tone we stand upon to touch the next.

Walter Chappell passed away in 2000 in Santa Fe, New Mexico.

Glossary

afferent: nerves conveying impulses inward to the central nervous system.

ajsam: bodies: in Sufism, the plane constituted by subtle templates.

akhlaq Allah: the manner of God.

alchemical marriage: this stage begins the descent of spirit into incarnation; the fourth stage of the six-stage alchemical process

ali: eminent, noble, the most high.

anabolic: constructive metabolism in which simpler compounds are converted into more complex ones.

asma ilahi: the names of God, which are the qualities which form the basis of *wazifa* practice; in tradition there are ninety-nine names, though there are varying lists which, when combined, contain far more than ninety-nine.

ayat: signs, clues.

'azim: great, high in dignity, enthusiastic.

'aziz: honored, beloved.

baqa: subsistence; the stage following fana .

basit: the spender, the expander.

batin: the veiled one, inner, hidden.

*baya*t: homage; the rite of initiation, sometimes referred to as "taking hand," making a pledge.

body of resurrection: what we would call the subtle body, relative to the dense or gross physical body; the vehicle we will inhabit when we leave the physical plane.

catabolic: destructive metabolism in which complex compounds are converted into simpler ones with the release of energy.

centrifugal: tending to fly off from the center.

centripetal: tending toward the center.

chakra; center of subtle energy in the body.

Chesed: mercy, power of love in the Kabbalistic tree of life.

creative imagination: the intermediary realm in which the encounter of God descending toward the creature and the creature ascending toward the Creator takes place.

dark night of the soul: a state of purification which the soul passes through on its journey to union with God.

dervish: Sufi practitioner.

Dhu'l Jalal wa'l-Ikram: the Lord of splendid power.

efferent: nerves conveying impulses outward from the central nervous system.

explicate: the state of unfoldment, the revelation of the implicit, the explanation of the implied.

fana: the annihilation of the false self.

Gevurah: power, mastery in the Kabbalistic tree of life.

hadi: the guide.

hadith: traditional sayings attributed to the Prophet Muhammad.

hahut: the transcendent plane.

haqq: Truth.

hayy: life energy.

hazrat: presence, dignity; title of respect of a Sufi master.

hidden treasure: metaphor for the being of God, or the soul, which is veiled from the physical senses.

hologram: a three-dimensional image.

holomovement: an unbroken and undivided totality which carries an implicate order within it, and from which this implicate order emerges and returns.

imkan: all-possibility.

implicate: covert, inverted.

'ishq Allah: the divine nostalgia, love of God.

jabarut: the plane of splendor.

Kabbalah: generally applied to the many forms of Jewish mysticism.

lahut: the plane of archetypes.

latif: delicate, subtle, graceful.

malakut: the celestial plane.

maya: illusion.

mithal: the plane of metaphor.

muhasaba: the examination of conscience.

muhaymin: the protector.

muhyi: the quickener, the giver of life.

mu'id: the restorer.

murshid: the guide; senior Sufi teacher.

nasut: the physical plane.

pir: the elder; a Sufi spiritual director.

pir-o murshid: this title unites the roles of murshid and pir.

qahir: sovereign.

qasab: breathing practice that strengthens and balances the breath.

quddus: pure spirit, Holy Spirit.

rahim: merciful, compassionate.

rahman: beneficent, magnanimous.

samadhi: meditative absorption; the highest stage of Yoga as taught by Patanjali.

sannyasin: a Hindu ascetic.

satori: the experience of enlightenment in Buddhism.

shagal: a Sufi breathing practice.

smiling forehead: an expression derived from the Persian, in which forehead means expression; having a bright and optimistic attitude toward life.

subtle body: a level of our being less dense than the physical world and hence not apparent to the senses.

vairagya: path of indifference.

Vedanta: the philosophy of the Upanishads.

wali: master.

wasi: all-embracing.

wazifa (plural, *waza'if*): a form of meditation practice comparable to use of a mantra

zahir: manifest, appearant, revealed in epiphany.

zikr: remembrance; in Sufism, the ritual of divine remembrance.

Bibliography

Addas, Claude, *The Quest for the Red Sulphur: The Life of Ibn '
Arabi*, Cambridge: Islamic Textx Society, 1993.

'Attar, Fariduddin. *The Conference of the Birds*. Trans. R. P.
Masani. London: Oxford University Press, 1924.

Bohm, David. *Unfolding Meaning*. London: Routledge, 1988.

———. *Wholeness and the Implicate Order*. London: Routledge,
1983.

Burckhardt, Titus. *Alchemy: Science of the Cosmos, Science of the
Soul*. Trans. William Stoddart. Dorset: Element Books,
1986.

Capra, Frithjof. *The Tao of Physics*. Boston: Shambhala, 1985.

Corbin, Henry. *Creative Imagination in the Sufism of Ibn Arabi*.
Trans. Ralph Manheim. Princeton: Princeton University
Press, 1969.

Gibran, KahliL *The Prophet*. New York: Alfred Knopf, 1923.

Herrigel, Eugene. *Zen in the Art of Archery*. New York: Pantheon
Books, 1953.

al-Hujwiri, Ali Ibn Uthman al-Jullabi. *Kashf al Mahjub*. Trans.
Reynold Nicholson. Cambrige: Gibb Memorial, 1936.

Ibn 'Arabi, Muhyiddin. *The Bezels of Wisdom*. Trans. R. J. W.
Austin. Ramsey, NJ: Paulist Press, 1980.

———. *Journey to the Lord of Power: A Sufi Manual on Retreat*.
Trans. Rabia Terri Harris. New York: Inner Traditions,
1981.

———. *The Tarjuman al Ashwaq: A Collection of Mystical Odes*.
Trans. Reynold Nicholson. London: Theosophical
Publishing House, 1978.

———. *What the Seeker Needs*. Trans. Tosun Bayrak and Rabia
Terri Harris. Putney, VT: Threshold Books, 1992.

225

Jilani, 'Abd al-Qadir. *Utterances*. Trans. Muhtar Holland. Houston: Al-Baz Publishing, 1992.

al-Junayd. *The Life, Personality and Writings of al Junayd*. Ed. and trans. Ali Hassan Abdel-Kader. London: Luzac & Co., 1976.

Jung, Carl. *Memories, Dreams, Reflections*. New York: Random House, 1961.

———. *Synchronicity*. Trans. R. F. C. Hull. Princeton: Princeton University Press, 1973.

Khan, Inayat. *The Alchemy of Happiness*. Vol. 6. *The Sufi Message of Hazrat Inayat Khan*. Katwijk: Servire, 1978.

———. *The Art of Being and Becoming*. New Lebanon: Omega Publications, 1982.

———. *The Awakening of the Human Spirit*. New Lebanon, NY: Omega Publications, 1982.

———. *The Complete Sayings*. New Lebanon, NY: Omega Publications, 2010.

———. *Gayan, Vadan, Nirtan*. New Lebanon, NY: Sulūk Press 2015.

———. *Healing and the Mind World*. Vol. 4. *The Sufi Message of Hazrat Inayat Khan*. Katwijk: Service, 1982

———. *In an Eastern Rose Garden*. Vol. 7. *The Sufi Message of Hazrat Inayat Khan*. Katwijk: Servire, 1979.

———. *The Inner Life*. Vol. 1, *The Sufi Message of Hazrat Inayat Khan Centennial Edition*. New Lebanon, NY: Suluk Press, 2015.

———. *Mastery Through Accomplishment*. New Lebanon, NY: Omega Publications, 1978.

———. *The Mysticism of Sound*. Vol. 2, *The Sufi Message of Hazrat Inayat Khan Centennial Edition*. Richmond: Suluk Press, 2017.

———. *Philosophy, Psychology, Mysticism*. Vol. 11. *The Sufi Message of Hazrat Inayat Khan,* Katwijk: Service, 1979.

———. *Song of the Prophets: The Unity of Religious Ideals* New Lebanon, NY: Omega Publications 2009.

————. *Spiritual Liberty*. Vol. 5. *The Sufi Message of Hazrat Inayat Khan.* Katwijk: Service, 1979.

————. *Sufi Mysticism, The Path of Initiation*. Vol. 10. *The Sufi Message of Hazrat Inayat Khan* Katwijk: Servire, 1979

————. *Sufi Teachings*. Vol. 8. *The Sufi Message of Hazrat Inayat Khan.* London: Barrie & Jenkins, 1962.

————. *Sufi Teachings*. Rev. ed. Dorset: Element Books, 1991.

————. "Supplementary Papers." Unpublished.

————. *The Vision of God and Man*. Vol. 12. *The Sufi Message of Hazrat Inayat Khan* Katwijk: Servire, 1982.

Khan, Pir Vilayat. *The Call of the Dervish*. New Lebanon, NY: Omega Publications, 1981.

————. *The Ecstasy Beyond Knowing: A Manual of Meditation*. New Lebanon, NY: Suluk Press, 2014.

————. *Introducing Spirituality into Counseling and Therapy*. New Lebanon, NY: Omega Publications, 1982.

————. *The Message in Our Time: The Life and Teaching of the Sufi Master Pir-O Murshid Inayat Khan*. New Lebanon: Omega Publications, 2003.

Massignon, Louis. *The Passion of al-Hallaj*. 4 vols. Trans. Herbert Mason. Princeton: Princeton University Press, 1982.

Neumann, Erich. *The Origins and History of Consciousness*. Princeton: Princeton University Press, 1970.

Poincaré, Henri. *Science and Hypothesis*. New York: The Science Press, 1905.

Prigogine, Ilya. *From Being to Becoming: Time and Complexity in the Physical Sciences*. New York: Freeman, 1980.

Pirgogine, Ilya, and Isabelle Stengers. *Order Out of Chaos*. New York: Bantam Books, 1984.

Progoff, Ira. *Jung, Synchronicity, and Human Destiny: Non-Causal Dimensions of Human Experience*. New York: The Julian Press, 1963.

Rumi, Jalal ad-Din. *The Mathnawi of Jalaluddin Rumi*. Trans. Reynold Nicholson. Cambridge: Gibb Memorial, 1926.

————. *Mystical Poems of Rumi*. Trans. A. J. Arberry. Chicago:

University of Chicago Press, 1968.

———. *Mystical Poems of Rumi: Second Selection, Poems 201–400*. Trans. A. J. Arberry. Chicago: University of Chicago Press, 1991.

St. John of the Cross. *The Collected Works of St. John of the Cross*. Trans. Kieran Kavanaugh and Otilio Rodriguez. Washington DC: ICS Publications, 1969.

Scholem, Gershom. *Major Trends in Jewish Mysticism*. New York: Schocken Books, 1941.

Shabistari, Sa`duddin Mahmud. *The Secret Rose Garden*. Trans. Florence Lederer. Grand Rapids: Phanes Press, 1987.

Sheldrake, Rupert. *A New Science of Life*. London: Blond and Briggs, 1981.

———. *The Rebirth of Nature: The Greening of Science and God*. New York: Bantam Books, 1991.

Shepherd, Kevin. *A Sufi Matriarch: Haxrat Babajan*. Cambridge: Anthropographia, 1985.

Smith, Margaret. *The Persian Mystics: 'Attar*. London: John Murray, 1932.

Teilhard de Chardin, Pierre, *The Phenomenon of Man*. New York: Harper and Brothers, 1959.

Pir Vilayat Inayat Khan

Biographical Note

Pir Vilayat Inayat Khan (1916–2004) was the eldest son and spiritual successor of Hazrat Pir-O-Murshid Inayat Khan, the first Sufi master to teach in the West. Born in England, Vilayat Inayat Khan was educated at the Sorbonne, Oxford, and École Normale de Musique de Paris. During World War II he served in the British Royal Navy and was assigned the duties of mine sweeping during the invasion of Normandy. His sister Noor-un-Nisa Inayat Khan served in the French section of SOE as a radio operator. She was captured and later executed at Dachau concentration camp.

After the war, Pir Vilayat pursued his spiritual training by studying with masters of many different religious traditions throughout India and the Middle East. While honoring the initiatic tradition of his predecessors, in his teachings Pir Vilayat continually adapted traditional Eastern spiritual practices in keeping with the evolution of Western consciousness. Throughout his life, he was an avid student of many religious and spiritual traditions and incorporated the rich mystical heritage of East and West into his teachings, adding to it the scholarship of the West in music, science, and psychology. He taught in the tradition of Universal

Sufism, which views all religions as rays of light from the same sun.

Pir Vilayat initiated and participated in many international and interfaith conferences promoting understanding and world peace as well as convening spiritual and scientific leaders for public dialogues. In 1975 he founded the Abode of the Message in New Lebanon, New York, which served as the central residential community of the Sufi Order International,[1] a conference and retreat center, and a center of esoteric study. He also founded the Omega Institute for Holistic Studies, a flourishing learning center in Rhinebreck, New York. He published many books on aspects of meditation and realization.

---

1 Now known as the Inayati Order and based in Richmond, Virginia. www.inayatiorder.org

Index

A

Abraham 163

Abu'l-Hasan al-Hujwiri. 183–184

addiction 18, 164, 202. *See also* drug.

adrenal glands 81

afferent nerves 174, 221

ajsam 112, 176, 192, 221; *ajsam* level 131. *See also* astral plane.

akashic body 167, 170–171

akhlaq Allah 55, 222

Aladdin 52

alchemy xiv, 52, 190; alchemical marriage 74, 168, 221. *See also* coagulate, distillation.

al-Hallaj *See* Husayn ibn Mansur Hallaj.

'ali 152

al-Junayd 193

all-possibility 77, 81, 222; all-potentiality 77–78, 117–118. *See also imkan.*

amino acid chains 110, 154

anabolic 16, 221

ana'l-Haqq 54, 99. *See also haqq,* truth.

ananda samadhi 113

angels 115, 162, 194: angelic face 127, 165; fallen angel 95; mature angels 211; music of the angels 168; plane/sphere of the angels 96, 202, 107, 125, 211; singing with the angels 171; types of angels 126. *See also* archangel, celestial beings, celestial plane, *malakut.*

anger 24, 55, 97, 146, 149, 152–153

antipodes 31, 108

Arabic language 156

archangel 162. *See also* individual archangels by name.

archery 184

archetypes 52, 53, 117, 136, 176; level of archetypes 99, 117, 157, 223. *See also* ideal, *lahut,* names of God, qualities, *wazifa.*

aristocracy of the soul and the democracy of the ego 39, 41, 208

asamprajnata samadhi 110

asanas 20

asma ilahi 9, 134, 221. *See also* names, *wazifa.*

asmita 117. *See also jabarut.*

astral plane 91; astral travel 52, 191. *See also ajsam.*

atom 84, 101, 121, 142, 158, 160

'Attar *See* Farid ad-Din 'Attar.

attunement 4–5, 56, 58, 82, 96, 120, 126–129, 146, 153, 157–160, 164, 169–172, 175, 195–197, *(cont. overleaf)*

responsibility.
consciousness xiv, 5, 13, 15,
19–20, 24, 26, 29, 34,
37, 56, 59, 62, 71, 74,
88–91, 93, 96–97,
99–105, 107, 110,
113–114, 125, 139,
142–143, 145, 147,
152, 163, 168–170,
177, 190–191, 197,
198, 200, 201–202,
205, 207, 231; con-
sciousness of another
person 20, 26–28,
245, 147; conscious-
ness of teacher, master,
prophet 163, 202;
consciousness of the
universe 107; divine
consciousness 53;
embodying the states
of consciousness 120;
God-consciousness
203. *See also* awareness,
mind, psyche.
cosmic celebration 10, 95,
116, 126, 171
cosmos 1, 34, 116, 168–169,
219; cosmic dimension
79, 84–86, 88–89,
107, 122; cosmic
emotion 71, 114, 210;
cosmic energy 16;
magnetic field of the
cosmos 68. *See also*
cosmic celebration,
earth, galaxies, heavens,
moon, outer space,
stars, sun, universe.

countenance 96, 120,
125–128, 130; angelic
countenance 162, 165,
176. *See also* face.
creativity 12, 20, 36, 59, 64–
65, 81–82, 113–114,
144, 159, 162, 165,
169, 179, 185, 195,
215–216; creative
imagination 14,
103–104, 106, 110,
113, 176, 222. *See also*
imagination, metaphor,
mithal, music, myth.
crown center 72, 75, 81
crystal 131, 149; crystalliza-
tion 166

D

dark night of the soul 39–40,
44, 114, 133, 222.
See also despair, soul,
suffering.
death 115, 130–131, 133,
191; meditation as a
preparation for death
192
defilement 4, 32, 45, 192–
193, 208
dervish 4, 114, 118, 140–141,
179, 183, 222; power
of the dervish 54. *See
also* Sufis.
descent through the spheres
75, 90, 127. *See also*
Holy Spirit.
desirelessness 104. *See also* detachment, indifference.
desire 99, 104–105, 176, 185

religious dogmas 108. *See also* Christianity, church, dogma, faith, Hindus, Jew, monks, temple.

reminiscences 23, 90, 92, 102, 115–116. *See also* memory, nostalgia.

renunciation 9, 41, 186. *See also* detachment, sacrifice.

repetition 23, 54, 134, 156–157, 159–160, 162–163. *See also* mantram, *wazifa*.

resilience 69, 130. *See also muid*.

resonance 28, 58, 62, 101, 131, 168, 200, 211, 179; sympathetic resonance 167. *See also* gong, sound, overtones, vibration.

responsibility xv, 4, 140–143, 183, 198, 200, 205. *See also* conscience, life situations.

resurrection 127, 130–131, 165, 192, 194, 221. *See also* rebirth.

retreat xi, xiii–xv, 3–6, 11, 17–19, 36, 39, 42, 44–45, 48, 50, 57, 59, 66, 95, 141, 146, 152, 160, 185, 189, 232. *See also khalwa*, solitude, silence.

revelation 4, 108–110, 112–113, 120, 145,

150–151, 153–154, 163, 181, 215, 222. *See also* insight, intuition, .

rhythm 15, 56, 67, 95; rhythm of breath 16

rishis 168

RNA 143

rudra vina 160, 168

S

sabija 117

sacredness 32, 125, 150–153, 197–198. *See also* sacrament, sanctum santorum.

sacrifice 203–204. *See also* renunciation.

sacrilege 150–151, 153

sacrament 151

saint 27, 115, 163–164; path of the saints 10. *See also* individual saints by name.

samadhi 58, 63, 74, 79, 86, 100–119, 132, 142, 190, 223; *ananda samadhi* 113; *nirvekara samadhi* 111, 113; *nirvetarka samadhi* 109, 110–111; *sarvikara samadhi* 111–112; *sarvitarka samadhi* 108, 111. *See also* awakening, bliss, ecstasy, enlightenment, illumination, niravana, satori.

sanctimony 153, 196, 208

sanctum sanctorum 75

truthfulness 30, 49, 123, 134–137; ultimate truth 118. *See also haqq.*

U

U-boats 144

unconscious 37, 42, 71, 81, 157

unfoldment xiv, 11, 17, 132, 222

unity 14, 24, 26, 50, 53–54, 63, 76, 99, 118, 176; divine unity 17. *See also hahut,* totality.

universe 4, 9, 12–17, 45, 47, 50, 61–62, 64, 71, 75, 77–78, 84, 88–90, 95, 100, 107–109, 112, 114, 117, 141, 148–149, 158–159, 161, 166, 170–171, 179, 181, 187–191, 198, 207, 210; energy that moves the universe 70, 123; fabric of the universe 92; intention behind the universe 87; language of the universe 158; laws of the universe 181; light of the universe 78, 121–123, 162, 169; meaning behind the universe 158; mechanism of the universe 30; nostalgia of the universe 16; original state of the universe 158; potentialities of the universe 56; programming behind the universe 86, 97, 188–189; reprogramming of the whole universe 14; software of the universe 6–7, 14, 176; sound of the universe 161, 168, 170; splendor beyond the universe 176; subjacent universes 123; thinking of the universe 94, 107–108, 117, 190; universe as a being 107. *See also* cosmos, earth, galaxies, moon, outer space, planet, stars, sun.

unknowing 13, 90, 188

unmasking 9, 62, 100, 106, 115. *See also* illusion, mask, maya, veil.

V

vacuum 30, 63–64, 73–74, 77, 176–177. *See also* void.

vairagya 17, 66, 105, 199, 223. *See also* detachment, freedom, indifference, renunciation.

values 132, 204–205; scale of values 58–60. *See also* ideals.

Vedanta 86, 99, 106, 223. *See also* Hinduism.

veil 10, 47, 56, 154, 222; veiled one 56, 66, 153, 221; *(cont. overleaf)*